AS/A Level Study Guide

Developing the Skills for
A Level History

R. Paul Evans

AS/A Level Study Guide
Developing the Skills of the A Level Historian

© Aberystwyth University, 2009

Published by CAA, Aberystwyth University, The Old College,
King Street, Aberystwyth, SY23 2AX (http://www.caa.aber.ac.uk).
Sponsored by the Welsh Assembly Government.

ISBN: 978 1 84521 315 2

Editor: Lynwen Rees Jones
Designer: Arwel Thomas/Argraff
Illustrator: Chris Saunderson
Printers: Cambrian Printers, Aberystwyth

Acknowledgements
CAA would like to thank the following for permission to
reproduce materials in this publication:

Cadw, Welsh Assembly Government (Crown Copyright) – p. 70
bottom, 88 top; Darlow Smithson – p. 45; David King Collection –
p.56 centre & bottom; David Low/Solo Syndication/Associated
Newspapers Ltd – p.48; English Heritage Photo Library – p.81;
Flintshire Archive – p.52 top; Getty Images – p.47; Gomer – p.52
bottom; Gwasg Gee (extract from *Gwae Awdur Dyddiaduron* by R.
Williams Parry (adaptation)) – p.5; Harper Collins (extract from
William Pitt the Younger by William Hague) – p.42; Indus Films – p.88
bottom; Courtesy of Ken Marschall.com – p.44 bottom; Macmillan
(extract from *What is History?* by E. H. Carr) – p.75; National
Library of Wales – p.58, 84; National Museum Wales – p.70 top &
centre; New York Public Library – p.44 top; Pearson Education –
p.41 right; Penguin Group (UK) – p.41 left; Punch Ltd. – p.49;
TopFoto – p.5, 6, 44 centre, 46, 50, 72, 77, 80, 82, 83, 87; University
of Wales Press – p.18.

Every effort has been made to trace and acknowledge ownership
of copyright. The publishers will be pleased to make suitable
arrangements with any copyright holders who have not been
contacted.

Thank you to Siwan Evans, Richard Drew, Aled James and Meinir
Jones for their valuable guidance.

Thank you also to the following schools for taking part in the
trialling process:
Ysgol Bro Myrddin, Carmarthen
Ysgol Dyffryn Ogwen, Bethesda
Mold Alun School, Mold
Fairwater High School, Cwmbran

A Welsh medium version of this publication is also available.

Contents

CHAPTER ONE

STUDYING HISTORY AT AS AND A LEVEL:

An introduction

What is history?

The Oxford English Dictionary defines **History** as 'the chronological record or narrative of past events'. It is a written account detailing events in their order of time and may refer to a particular country, people or individual. The person who records this account is defined as the **Historian**. However, as with all definitions, people have interpreted its meaning in different ways, as the following quotations illustrate.

For discussion:
Study the quotations listed below. Which of these, in your opinion, best describes the study of history? Explain your reasons.

Different interpretations of the study of history:

'History – a hardcore of interpretation surrounded by a pulp of disputable facts.'
E. H. Carr, an historian writing in the mid-twentieth century.

'What does History care about a saint or a satyr?
    She tells the truth, the whole truth? The whole?
Nearer than the historian to the unfailing truth
    Is the dramatist, who is all lies.'

The final lines of a sonnet, *Gwae Awdur Dyddiaduron (Woe to the author of diaries)*, composed by R. Williams Parry in 1939.

'History is the lie commonly agreed upon.'
Voltaire, an eighteenth century French philosopher and writer.

'The historian can learn much from the novelist.'
Samuel Eliot Morison, a twentieth century American historian.

'The history of all hitherto existing society is the history of class struggle.'

Karl Marx, German social philosopher and revolutionary who founded modern Socialism and Communism. Author of the Communist Manifesto (1848).

'History and myth are two aspects of a kind of grand pattern in human destiny: history is the mass of observable or recorded fact, but myth is the abstract or essence of it.'

Robertson Davies, a twentieth century Canadian novelist and playwright.

'What men have done and said; above all what they have thought – that is history.'
S. R. Maitland, a noted historian of the nineteenth century.

'History, a distillation of rumour.'
Thomas Carlyle, a nineteenth century Scottish essayist and historian.

'The past is malleable and flexible, changing as our recollection interprets and re-explains what has happened.'

Peter Berger, a Professor of Sociology and Theology at Boston University during the late twentieth century.

'History is more or less bunk.'

Henry Ford, car manufacturer who created the Ford Motor Company in 1903.

All these quotations serve to illustrate that history is open to a great deal of interpretation and this is one of the key characteristics of the study of history at both AS and A level. While certain facts will be accepted as irrefutable, such that Henry Tudor became king following his defeat of Richard III at the Battle of Bosworth in 1485, debate will always surround the interpretation of the events of that day. Why did the Stanley brothers, for example, decide to switch their allegiance at the last minute and side with Henry Tudor against the Yorkist King? Historians will always argue and debate about why a particular event occurred at a particular time; why it followed the path it did and what the consequences were of that event. They will debate whether the traditional view of the causes and consequences of that event are really correct; are the causes placed in their correct order and is the author of this version of events accurate in his/her interpretation? Does the historian denote a particular bias in their interpretation?

These and many other questions will form the basis of your study of history at AS/A Level. It is a course that will involve you in a great deal of debate about the evidence you are studying, about the accuracy of the interpretations and representations you are presented with and about the reliability and motive of the authors who composed those pieces of evidence.

For discussion:
(a) What do you think Karl Marx meant when he said that the history of human society is really the history of class struggle?

(b) Study the quotations by E. H. Carr, Voltaire and Peter Berger. Can you detect any similarities in their views of what history is?

(c) What do you think Samuel Eliot Morison meant when he said the historian has much to learn from the novelist?

(d) Would you agree or disagree with Henry Ford's view that 'history is more or less bunk'?

What are the differences between GCSE and AS/A Level history?

- **Studying the past in much greater depth** – a larger percentage of your timetable will now be given over to the study of history which will allow for more in-depth analysis and evaluation of events, together with their causes and consequences;

- **Working independently** – you will be expected to undertake more research and investigation on your own and there will be a great deal of emphasis upon independent learning;

- **Demonstrating the skills of the historian at a more sophisticated level** – you will need to demonstrate a greater depth of factual knowledge and understanding, display more advanced skills of source analysis and evaluation, place events into their historical context and deal with historical interpretations;

- **Need to avoid narrative** – you will be expected to develop good analytical and evaluative writing skills; an answer that displays a heavy concentration of narrative might have scored you high marks at GCSE but it will not do so at AS/A level;

- **The selection and organisation of material** – to answer questions at AS/A level you will need to demonstrate the ability to select, arrange and prioritise information to ensure that it answers a particular question;

- **Extended writing is more important** – you will be expected to write essays, both structured and open-ended, which display a structured and well supported argument in answer to a particular question;

- **Greater emphasis upon source evaluation skills** – you will need to demonstrate your ability to analyse, evaluate and reach a sustained judgement about the value of historical sources;

- **Mastering specific historical vocabulary** – you will need to show an understanding of key historical terms particular to the period you are studying such as 'totalitarian', 'radical', 'nationalist', 'the bourgeoisie' and 'proletariat';

- **Mastering more specific terminology used in question setting** – understanding the meaning of key command words in the question such as 'discuss', 'to what extent', 'how important was' or 'how successful was?'

The study of both AS and A Level history is certainly more demanding that it was at GCSE but this incline in difficulty will only mirror the academic maturity that you will demonstrate during your sixth form or college studies.

What specific skills are examiners looking for at AS/A Level?

Examination Boards / Awarding Bodies
At the end of your two-year course in history your A Level certificate will be awarded by one of the following Examination Boards:

AQA CCEA Edexcel OCR WJEC

Whatever Examination Board sets the questions for the course you are studying at AS/A Level they will follow a set of assessment criteria known as Assessment Objectives. There are two Assessment Objectives, known as AO1 and AO2, each of which is sub-divided into part (a) and part (b). These are designed to test specific skills as set out in the following chart:

Assessment Objectives in History

AO1a recall, select and deploy historical knowledge appropriately, and communicate knowledge and understanding of history in a clear and effective manner;

AO1b demonstrate understanding of the past through explanation, analysis and arriving at substantiated judgements of:

- Key concepts such as causation, consequence, continuity, change and significance within an historical context;

- The relationships between key features and characteristics of the periods studied;

AO2a as part of an historical enquiry, analyse and evaluate a range of appropriate source material with discrimination;

AO2b analyse and evaluate, in relation to the historical context, how aspects of the past have been interpreted and represented in different ways.

It is important that you understand what these essential skills are and what they mean. The next three chapters will concentrate upon each of these Assessment Objectives in depth, allowing you to develop, practice and reinforce the skills necessary to secure a good grade in history at both AS and A Level.

Developing an understanding of the key concepts examined in history

Underpinning all the Assessment Objectives are the key concepts of history. These are the building blocks upon which the courses you will study are based, and it is therefore important that you comprehend and demonstrate a clear understanding and awareness of these key concepts.

(a)   Cause and consequence

While cause and consequence are often quoted together, it is important to remember that what lies between them is the effect. The cause of an event produces an effect (the event itself) and this in turn results in a consequence.

(i) Cause

A cause is a reason why something happened. In the majority of instances there is more than one cause and these can be broken up into long-term and short-term causes. You would be expected to identify this distinction and it is more than likely that you would be required to prioritise the causes, determining which are the more important and why.

E.g. Attitudes to woman in Britain began to change during the late Victorian and Edwardian era, the result being that women were granted the right to vote in 1918. You might be asked to identify the causes of this change of attitude and to ascertain the extent to which the First World War, for example, was the most important cause, which secured this political change.

(ii) Consequence

A consequence is what happened because of an action, it is the result of an event. As with causes, the consequences can be divided up into immediate results and long-term results. It is more than likely that you would be expected to identify the consequences of a particular event, rank them into some sort of order, determine whether they were immediate or long-term consequences, and possibly say why one might be seen as more important in relation to the others. It requires you to develop a rational argument in support of your judgement.

E.g. A consequence of how the Second World War ended in 1945 and the position of the Allied powers at that particular point in time, was the division of Europe into East and West. Uncertainty and mistrust among the Allied leaders resulted in a sharp political division, Communism versus Capitalism, which in turn resulted in a sharp military division, NATO versus the Warsaw Pact. The consequence of all these differences was the beginnings of the Cold War.

Your task

Identify an event you have recently studied. Break down that event into its three phases – causes, the event itself and its consequences. Within each of the causes and consequences phases sub-divide the key issues according to their importance or significance, giving a reason for your rank order.

(b)   Continuity and change

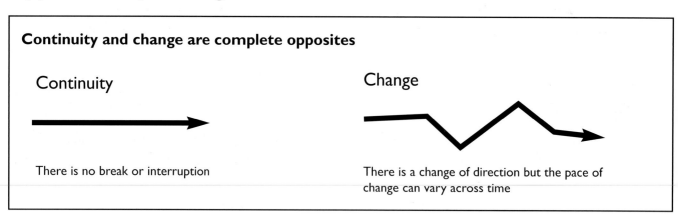

Continuity and change are complete opposites

Continuity

There is no break or interruption

Change

There is a change of direction but the pace of change can vary across time

(i) Continuity

Continuity is said to occur when things stay the same, there is no break or interruption. Unlike change, it is often harder to identify continuity and to explain why things have not changed. The measurement of continuity will be determined by the time span you are asked to consider. It may be a short period such as a decade or just a few years or, alternatively, it could be a much longer period such as a century or several centuries.

E.g. A study of punishment across several centuries. The operation of the Assize Courts continued without any significant changes from the time of conception during the reign of Henry II in the 1150s to their eventual reform in 1971 when they were replaced by the introduction of Crown Courts. They thus had over 800 years of continuity in terms of their identity and function.

(ii) Change

This is when something happens to make things different. The occurrence of that change can be rather sudden and take place within a relatively short time span or it can be more gradual, taking shape over a longer period of time. The nature of the change can also vary, the change can be very dramatic, marking a stark contrast to what went before or it could be gradual and piecemeal in nature. Very often the changes do not proceed at a uniform pace but oscillate between fast and slow rather like a foot on the accelerator pedal. The vehicle is moving forward but the speed will vary according to circumstances encountered on the road.

E.g. A study of the changing relationship between Wales and England during the medieval period. This very much depended upon the circumstances of the time. A strong English king such as Henry II or Edward I could keep the Welsh princes in check and thwart their ambitions of expansion. However, during periods when the power of the English crown was less strong such as the reign of Henry III or during periods of a resurgence of Welsh power under a strong prince such as Llywelyn the Great or Owain Glyndwr, English power was much reduced and the weighting of that relationship between Wales and England was reversed.

Sometimes you might be given an exercise to identify both continuity and change across the period of time.

E.g. A study of Peter the Great and his policy of Westernisation in Russia between 1696 and 1725. Questions relating to the reign of Peter the Great usually ask you to identify the changes that took place during his reign to usher in Westernisation and to assess the degree to which these were completely new changes and therefore constitute a radical departure from past tradition, or were they a continuation of policies begun by his immediate predecessors.

Your task

(a) Think back to your GCSE History course and identify an issue that demonstrated a period of continuity, suggesting the reasons for this continuity.

(b) Attempt the same process again but this time select a period that witnessed change, explaining why this change occurred.

(c)   The relationship between the key features and characteristics of a period

At AS and A Level you will be expected to demonstrate an understanding of the dominant features and characteristics of the period you are studying, and how they relate to one another. Do these features share common characteristics or are they distinctly different, and if so why? The skill that is being tested is your ability to detect and explain similarities and differences in the period under investigation.

> **E.g.** The nineteenth century witnessed a wave of revolutions associated with the rise of nationalism across Europe especially in the year 1848. In both the Italian and German states the revolutions of 1848 failed to shake off the shackles of overlordship from the Austro-Hungarian Empire. Yet during the 1860s and 1870s both these regions were able to secure independence and create their own nation states. You might be asked to consider why the attempts at unification failed in 1848 but succeeded a generation later, and whether the process of securing that unification was the same in Germany as it was in Italy.

> **(i) Similarity:** This will involve you identifying issues that are the same, that share common features and characteristics.

> **(ii) Difference:** This will involve you identifying things that are different, whether they are complete opposites or exhibit a less obvious degree of difference.

> **E.g.** You may be asked to consider how Hitler and Roosevelt dealt with the economic problems of the 1930s. They both came to power when their countries were experiencing the full force of the Great Depression and their first task was to tackle the effects of the economic downturn. Both pumped large sums of public money into the economy to create employment opportunities through the building of roads, public buildings such as schools and hospitals, and land reclamation schemes such as the planting of millions of trees. Hitler took this a step further and introduced conscription into the armed forces. Both men introduced measures to control big business and had to deal with the problem of trade unions. But here the similarities ended and some of their other policies were very different. America remained firmly isolationist and refused to spend vast sums on the armed forces, while Germany spent heavily on rearmament and began to embark upon an expansionist foreign policy during the mid-1930s.

(d)   The significance of historical context.

Demonstrating an understanding of historical context is an important skill at AS and A Level. In this instance context refers to the general setting, relating the event under investigation to the bigger picture, examining what is going on around it. It is a skill usually assessed in relation to the analysis and evaluation of a given historical source. It will involve you relating the source to what went on before and after the event, and assessing the degree to which the source provides a full or partial picture of the event.

> **E.g.** The source may refer to a specific cause of an event and you will be asked to assess its usefulness to the historian in understanding the reasons why this event happened. The source may only provide one cause and you will be expected to link it to the bigger picture and identify any other causes that are missing. In order to provide this context you will need to demonstrate a sophisticated level of knowledge and understanding of the period.

For discussion:
When studying the accomplishments of a celebrated individual such as Nelson Mandela or Martin Luther King can you give an accurate evaluation of their achievements without linking your investigation to the study of what was going on around them at that time?

Your task

(a)   Copy and complete the following diagram to illustrate and explain the key concepts examined in history at AS/A level.

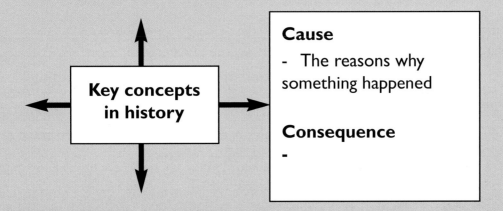

(b)   Explain why it is so important to study an event in its historical context.

Adapting to the demands of AS and A Level study

As previously stated there is a fundamental difference between the way history is studied at GCSE compared to AS and A Level. One of the major differences between your former GCSE timetable and your new AS timetable is that it now includes 'study periods' during which you will not be formally taught but will be expected to undertake some form of private study. As an historian this is the time that you will engage in independent research and investigation. A key element of this will be the undertaking of additional reading in order to build up your knowledge and understanding and so facilitate your ability to provide historical context.

A consequence of any additional reading will be the need to make your own notes. Such notes may be taken from books, articles from academic journals or, as is increasingly the case, from information downloaded from the Internet. Chapter Two will focus on how you will use this material to write essays, while Chapter Three will consider the usefulness and reliability of the information depending upon its origin. The following section will help give you guidance on how to undertake this initial note-making process.

1. Initial research

(a) Working from the general to the specific

Your first task is to locate suitable books or Internet sites from which you can obtain appropriate notes to help you understand the topic you are investigating. When locating such information it is always better to start with general history books, which will provide you with a good overview of the period. General histories will pick out the key characteristics and features of a period and provide a useful summary of them. This will enable you to start with a good grasp of the bigger picture. Once you have mastered the basics you can then proceed to investigate more deeply by reading more specialised texts.

Example of progression in your research and reading

You have been set an essay to investigate the causes of the Industrial Revolution in north Wales in the eighteenth century. You could divide up your reading and note making as follows:

General study: *A History of Wales 1660-1815*, by E. D. Evans (University of Wales Press, 1976). This contains a single chapter on industrial developments, which provides an overview of the major changes in each key industry.

↓

More specialised study: *The Industrial Revolution in North Wales*, by A. H. Dodd (University of Wales Press, 1933). This will contain specific chapters dealing with each key industry such as slate, copper, iron, coal and cotton.

↓

Specific study: *The Copper King: A biography of Thomas Williams of Llanidan*, by J. R. Harris (Liverpool University Press, 1964). This is a specific study of the development of the copper industry in Wales, concentrating upon mining activity on Anglesey and on developments in the smelting processes at Holywell and Swansea, all of which fell under the charge of Thomas Williams, Wales's first industrial millionaire.

At each stage you will have increased the depth and detail of your study.

> **Tip**
>
> **Each chapter will have its own bibliography, which will point you towards more detailed sources of information.**

Your task

When you next write an essay complete the chart below as a record of your research and preparation work. Aim to repeat this process for all future essays.

General history books / websites
More specific books / websites
Books by historians who are authorities in the field

(b)   Keep a record of the works consulted

When making notes from a book you should always record the title of the book, its author, together with the date and place of publication. You may need to follow up your notes at a later date and it is recommended that you record the exact page numbers alongside your notes. Such information will enable you to compile a bibliography and this is often required at the end of an essay.

What is a bibliography?

This is a list of books relating to a particular topic under investigation. It is usually arranged alphabetically according to the surname of the author and should include the full title of the publication, the name of the publisher and the date of publication. In the case of an article the name of the journal from which it is taken will be cited, together with its volume number and its year of publication. If the article has been downloaded from the Internet then the full http. web address should be provided.

Example:

Book:
Hughes, L. *Peter the Great: A Biography* (Yale, 2004).

Article:
Grey, I. 'Peter the Great in England' *History Today, 6* (1956), pp.225-34.

Website:
Trueman, C. *'Peter the Great'*
http://www.historylearningsite.co.uk/peter_the_great.htm

2. Making notes

Making notes is often seen as a chore, a time-consuming process that in today's world of fast technology is considered to be rather boring and out-dated. However, a good set of notes can make all the difference and provide you with the essential ingredients to write an informed and developed essay or to improve factual knowledge and understanding. It is easy to research using the Internet, to locate the desired information and to press the print button. For many students the printing process signifies that the work is done but in reality a page of printed notes is useless to you unless you read it with care and pick out the salient points.

Why make notes?

• You may have borrowed a book from a library and need to return it;

• Making notes will force you to read the chapter of the book with care and require you to decide what to write down and how to say it;

- The process of making notes helps you to make sense of what you read and so provide you with a better understanding;

- The concentration required to make notes will help to reinforce your knowledge and understanding of the period – you will be amazed by what you have sub-consciously remembered when you come to read these notes at a later date;

- Good note making provides you with a concise summary of the key features of a chapter and this will aid the later revision process.

The process of note making:

- Start by asking yourself why you are making these notes. Are they to provide research for an essay or to help build up a broader knowledge and understanding of the topic you are studying? Once you have decided on the purpose then this will determine the material you record and the order in which you record it.

- The first stage of note making is to skim-read the chapter. This will provide you with an overview of the main arguments or interpretations.

- As you read you may wish to underline key words or sentences, or highlight them with fluorescent marker. This will focus your attention on the text and enable you to pick out the main points. This is fine if you are working from a photocopy or computer printout but you may not wish to mark an actual textbook in this manner. Should this be the case then coloured 'post it' notes or 'stickies' are useful to enable you to record the key points or to act as bookmarks, which bullet point the key points discussed on that page.

- Re-read the chapter, making notes as you proceed. It is important they you keep your notes brief and, if possible, write them in your own words. You may wish to record them as a series of bullet points, breaking the notes up into clearly defined sections using sub-headings.

- As the notes are only for your own benefit it will save you time if you adopt short-hand and use abbreviations for frequent and key words. Some abbreviations are obvious such as GB for Great Britain or *Ind. Rev.* for Industrial Revolution, while others might be more obscure and particular to you. Whatever the abbreviation it is important that you remember what it means when you come to read your notes at a later date. However, you must never use abbreviations in any written work that is to be formally assessed. Abbreviations must be for your private use only.

Example of A Level note making

The following passage describes the opening stages of the Civil War in 1642 pertaining to Wales. It is taken from a book by Hugh Thomas, *A History of Wales, 1485-1660*, (University of Wales Press, 1972), pages 205-07.

a) The first task is to read the passage, underlining (or highlighting) the key points as you do so:

'[Charles] marched west to the Welsh border to recruit men for his assault upon London. While he made his headquarters at Shrewsbury, and established a second base at Chester, to enlist men and money, the Prince of Wales was dispatched to Raglan to obtain support for the royalist cause in South Wales. By the early days of October Charles had doubled his strength and on the twelfth he marched out of Shrewsbury with an army of some 16,000 men, among them a substantial number of Welshmen from the north and south. The earl of Essex with the parliamentary army, which had meanwhile been lying idle in and around Worcester, was slow to take up the pursuit, but overtook the king's army near Keynton at the base of Edgehill. Here was fought the first battle of the Civil War. The Welsh royalists, ill armed and untrained, played an inglorious part in the battle – many were killed and many more deserted. The indecisive outcome of the battle enabled the king to move on to Oxford and from here he advanced upon London. At Brentford the Welsh under Prince Rupert distinguished themselves in storming the enemy barricades, but a parliamentary show of strength at Turnham Green persuaded Charles to withdraw to Oxford. In the meantime, the marquis of Hertford, to whom the king had given supreme command in the west, had with the aid of the Raglan family recruited another army in South Wales. On 4 November he left Cardiff to join the king at Oxford, but he was overtaken at Tewkesbury by the earl of Stamford, the parliamentary governor of Hereford. In the battle that followed the Welsh royalists were again defeated with very heavy losses. Hertford was able to regroup his forces and take Hereford, which had been abandoned by Stamford, so that all was not lost. But the early engagements of the war had offered the Welsh cold comfort indeed.

Wales was important to the royalist cause. It was one of the king's most promising recruiting areas – the response to his early appeals had already shown this. It served to counter balance the Parliament-controlled east of England and offered him a strategic base for future military operations. Moreover, it offered easy access to Ireland where the king was already conducting negotiations for support in men and money. It was, therefore, vitally important for the king to control the border counties; equally it was to Parliament's advantage to seal Wales off. The struggle for control of the marches was inevitably a theatre of the war of considerable significance. At the outbreak of hostilities there was a fairly equal balance of strength in the region – the royalists with Chester, Shrewsbury, and other strong points controlled the northern part, while Parliament's hold upon Hereford, Gloucester, and Bristol gave them control in the south.

(b) Using the underlined notes as a guide you can now set about making your summary of the key points:

Ref: Hugh Thomas, *History of Wales, 1485-1660* (1972), pp.205-07

Welsh involvement in the first stages of the Civil War:

i.   Charles attempted to recruit support in Wales
        - Shrewsbury & Chester were bases in north
        - Raglan was base in south

ii.   12 Oct 1642 Charles left Shrewsbury with 16,000 men (inc. many Welshmen)
        - he met parliamentary army under Essex at Edgehill
        - was first battle of Civil War but was inconclusive
        - role of Welsh soldiers was not spectacular

iii.   Charles moved on to Oxford and London
        - Welsh forces met with better success at Brentford under Prince Rupert
        - but stronger Parliamentary forces caused Charles to retreat to Oxford

iv.   Marquis of Hertford raised another army in South Wales
        - his force defeated at Tewkesbury by Parliamentary force under Stamford
        - Hertford regrouped and was able to take Hereford

Importance of Wales to Charles:
i.   As a recruiting centre
ii.   Provided access to Ireland and possible support from there
iii.   Was vital for Charles to control border counties in north such as Chester and Shrewsbury as Parliament held the south such as Hereford, Gloucester & Bristol

Your task

Select a piece of writing (2 to 3 pages in length) from a textbook relating to your period of study. Attempt to summarise the main points as a series of bullet points.

3. Writing up

This is the final stage of the process but it cannot be completed successfully unless the previous background research and note making have been thorough. A good set of notes will provide the building blocks for your essay and your starting point should be to draft a plan to map out your essay. This will provide structure to your answer. You need to work out what to say in each paragraph and link it to the relevant sections in your notes. This can be a complex process and it is dealt with in much greater depth in the following chapter.

What skills will I take away from my study of AS/A Level History?

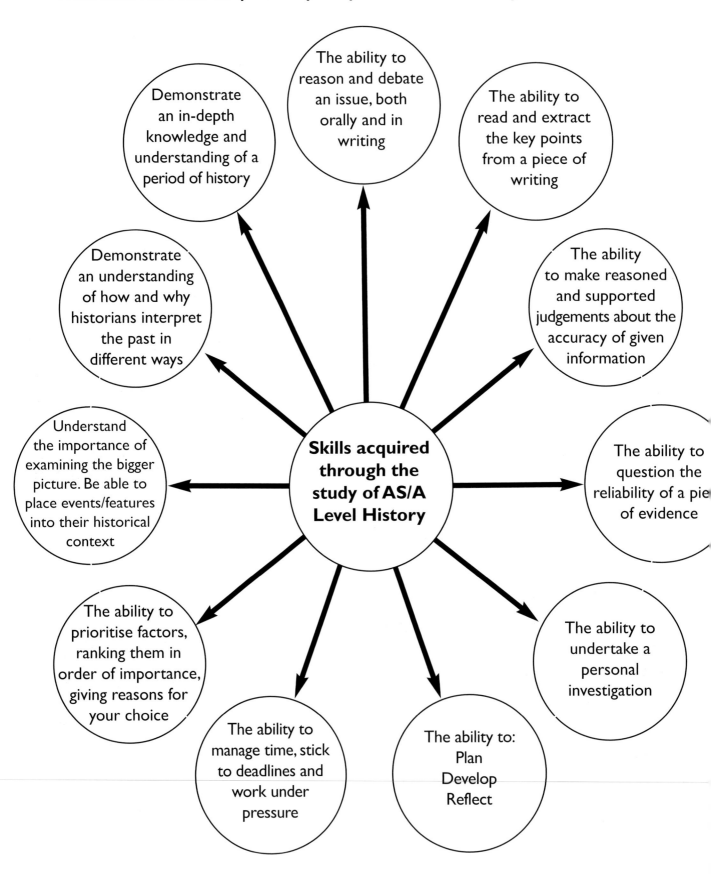

Through the study of history at AS and A level you will acquire a range of skills that will help you in your other subjects, in your future studies and in your eventual job. All these skills will be dealt with in some depth in the following chapters, and as you proceed through the sections you will be given the opportunity to develop and master these skills.

CHAPTER TWO

DEMONSTRATING THE SKILLS OF THE HISTORIAN

Extended writing: the structured essay and the open-ended essay question

The Essay Question

An essential requirement of any AS/A Level History course is the ability to demonstrate your historical knowledge and understanding of the topic and this is tested through the composition of an extended piece of writing in answer to a specific question. **Writing an essay is one of the best means of testing your comprehension of a topic**. It involves you selecting and reorganizing relevant material in order to produce a specific answer to a particular question. On the examination paper this piece of extended writing will usually take one of two forms: either the **structured essay** or the **open-ended essay question**.

Whatever the style of the essay question its purpose will be the same – to test your ability to write at length, often under timed conditions, in order to produced an informed, structured and reasoned answer. The question will have been designed to test two, sometimes three, of the Assessment Objectives listed below.

SUMMARY OF THE ASSESSMENT OBJECTIVES

AO1a – demonstrate your historical **knowledge and understanding**

AO1b – demonstrate your ability to **explain, analyse and reach a judgement**

AO2a – demonstrate your ability to **analyse and evaluate sources**

AO2b – demonstrate your understanding of **historical interpretations**

Most essay questions are specifically written to test Assessment Objectives 1a and 1b and, occasionally, 2b.

What makes a good essay?

There are three component parts to every essay you will write:

KEY PARTS TO THE ESSAY

INTRODUCTION ➡ DISCUSSION ➡ CONCLUSION

INTRODUCTION
- This is the opening section of the essay in which you need to introduce the topic and show an understanding of what the question is asking;
- You need to explain any key terms, names or dates mentioned in the question;
- You need to set the scene, outline your main lines of enquiry and identify any contrasting or counter arguments or interpretations.

DISCUSSION
- This is the main body of the essay in which you discuss the key issues raised in the introduction;
- You need to write a series of paragraphs, each one developing a key issue or line of enquiry;
- Each key issue or line of enquiry will need to be supported with relevant historical detail;
- The paragraphs need to follow in a logical order and they need to be linked together;
- There should be regular links back to the essay question to demonstrate that the information is relevant and that you are directly answering the essay question.

CONCLUSION
- This is where you finish off your answer;
- You need to round off your argument, referring back to the main points raised in the discussion section;
- You need to link the points together;
- It is very important that your conclusion contains a judgement which is both sustained and substantiated, and which links directly back to the essay question.

Throughout the whole process you will be required to argue a case, examining different sides to the argument and supporting this with relevant factual knowledge to illustrate and substantiate your lines of enquiry. Don't be too worried about whether there is a right or wrong answer, the most important aspect is whether you have selected appropriate information and constructed a logical argument to support your answer to the question. It is the style and consistency of the argument that carries the higher mark weighting rather than the factual content.

Remember

A good essay must read well and follow a logical sequence.

Analogy

In writing the essay you are acting like a barrister in court. The barrister is defending his/her client and has to convince the jury that the accused person did not commit the crime he/she has been charged with. In order to do this the barrister has to construct a case, presenting evidence to the jury to prove that the accused is not guilty of the charge. The jury will be unlikely to believe the barrister unless the case is well reasoned and is supported with proven factual detail.

In the same way a good essay will set out to reason the case, providing relevant historical detail to support the argument. You will need to demonstrate clear thinking and construct a well-supported argument. Just like the barrister will substantiate the case by calling witnesses to provide evidence, then a good essay will contain a range of factual detail to help support and prove the argument. In the same way the barrister has to prove a case so a good essay will require a sound argument supported with relevant facts and valid evidence. It will require an introduction, a reasoned discussion of the evidence, and a summing up in the form of a structured conclusion.

Remember that a barrister, who has prepared the case well and done the necessary research to find evidence to support the case, will have a better chance of convincing the jury. In the same way, if you have revised hard, performed the necessary background reading, set the event in its correct historical context and constructed a reasoned and well-supported argument, then you will be able to convince the examiner that your essay is deserving of marks in the top level of response.

A variant of the traditional open-ended A Level question is the structured question, which is more commonly asked at AS Level. The only difference between the two types of essay is that the structured question is broken up into two sub-sections. Although there might be two parts to the structured question it is usually **based upon one theme**. The first part is usually a descriptive type question, which is worth a lower mark allocation than the second part, which is more evaluative and analytical in its demands. It often requires you to make a judgement, ranking the causes, events or results of an event into an order of importance.

The skills needed to answer the structured question are the same as those needed to answer the open-ended essay question. You will need to plan your answer and argue well throughout both sections.

What types of essay questions are asked by the Examination Boards?

The various Examination Boards will tend to ask the same style of essay questions and the question will always be worded in such a way as to invite debate and analysis. All the questions will either start or end with important **command words**, which will guide the candidate as to how to answer the question. It is therefore very important that particular attention is paid to these **command words**.

Typical **command words** used in AS and A Level essay questions are as follows:

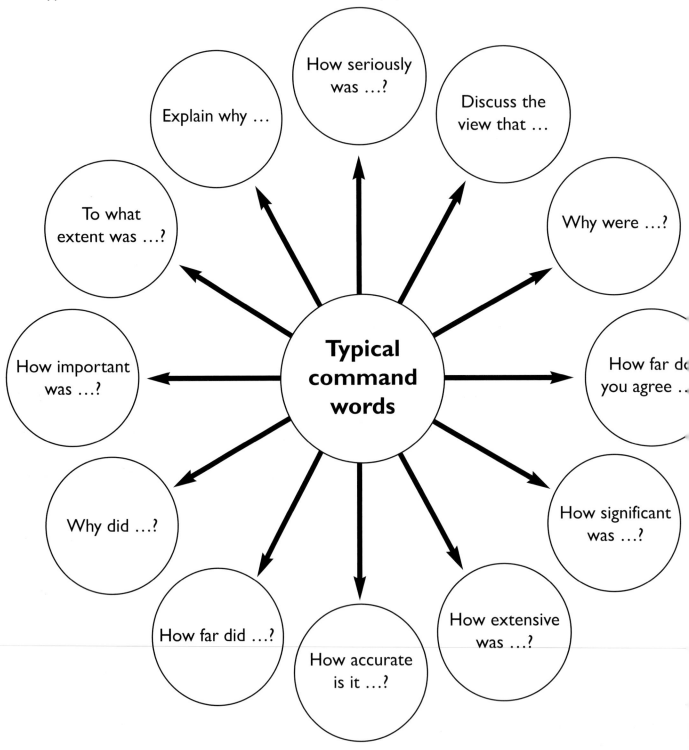

All these questions are **evaluative**. They require you to **weigh up the evidence, evaluating one factor against another** before reaching a **reasoned judgement**. This judgement, which needs to **demonstrate links back to the command words** in the question, must be **substantiated with specific factual knowledge** relating to the topic under investigation.

Examples of structured essay questions using these **command words**:

In the structured essay the question is usually divided into two sections: **part (a)**, which tends to be more descriptive, and **part (b)**, which is more analytical. Part (a) will carry a lower mark allocation than part (b).

Part (a) questions:
Explain why …

Part (b) questions:
To what extent …?
How important was …?
How significant was …?

Typical examples being:

1 (a) *Explain why* Frederick the Great invaded Silesia in 1740.

   (b) *To what extent was* the growth of Prussian power in this period mainly caused by her military strength?

2 (a) *Explain why* there was instability in the Balkans up to 1914.

   (b) *To what extent was* the Alliance System mainly responsible for the outbreak of the First World War?

Examples of open-ended essay questions using these command words:

How far was the collapse of the Liberal state in Italy caused by the First World War?

How important was William Wilberforce to the campaign to abolish British participation in the slave trade?

How significant was the role of John Wilkes in the revival of reform agitation in Britain in the 1760s and early 1770s?

To what extent was the rise of Parliament mainly responsible for the weakening power of the Crown by 1603?

Alternatively, the question might require an evaluation of a short quotation, in which case the command words will come after the quotation:

'Between 1933 and 1937, the British public's hostility to the confrontation of foreign powers left the National Government with no alternative to a policy of appeasing Hitler and Mussolini.' **How far do you agree with** this judgement?

'Social and economic conditions were always a factor, but rarely a trigger.' **Discuss this view of** the causes of rebellions in England and Ireland under the Tudors.

'The fear of Russia was the main driving force behind Britain's relationship with Europe between 1880-1980.' **Discuss this view.**

What do you need to do to answer these styles of essay questions?

Once you have selected the essay question you intend to answer you need to identify the command words. These will instruct you of the line of approach you need to adopt in your answer. Highlighting or circling them is often useful in helping you focus upon them.

The next step is to ascertain what the command words are actually asking you to do:

- '**Explain**' and '**why**' questions require you to identify a list of reasons, explaining how or why each contributed to the event named in the question.

- '**To what extent**' questions require you to give a judgement, having weighed up one factor against another.

- '**Assess**' and '**How important was**' or '**How successful was**' questions require you to make judgements supported by reasons, explanations and evidence. It often requires you to evaluate the named factor in the essay in relation to other factors.

- A '**quotation**', which is followed by '**Discuss**', requires you to clearly identify the issue at stake and produce a reasoned and well-supported response.

All these types of questions require an **investigative approach**. None of them requires a **narrative approach**. This is the essential difference between GCSE and A Level History – at GCSE you are rewarded for your factual knowledge and often the ability to 'tell the story' via good narrative is afforded a high number of marks. At AS/A Level this is not the case, and if you spend time writing lengthy narratives you will not score high marks, since this approach does not usually answer the question. Answers to essay questions have to be proven and follow a logical structure, each paragraph forming a logical progression to the argument. Like all your AS/A Level studies the art of essay writing will get easier with practice.

Remember

'**The ability to write good essays does not come to many people easily. It is a skill which requires constant attention and practice.**'

Dr Paul Hayward, History Lecturer, Lancaster University

Analogy

An eighteen year old student would not expect to pass his/her driving test without first having some practical driving lessons in which they learn and practice how to handle and manoeuvre the car. Such lessons are essential in order to understand and learn the basics of how to drive. Lack of thorough preparation means failure.

In the same manner an eighteen-year-old student should not expect to be proficient at essay writing without first having practiced beforehand. You cannot expect to go into the exam room and write a first class essay under timed conditions unless you have practiced the technique of writing under pressure. Practise enables you to find out your weaknesses such as bad timing or lack of factual knowledge, and allows you the opportunity to rectify these deficiencies before you sit the real thing. In this way you will be confident that whatever the question you can give of your best. Like the driving test, your aim should be to pass the test first time with flying colours.

Motto for success: *Practise regularly and be prepared.*

Tips for successful essay writing

Answering the structured essay question

Mark allocation:
Pay attention to the marks allocated for each part of the question. Part (a) is likely to carry substantially fewer marks than part (b) and therefore you should gauge the length of your answer accordingly. If part (a) is worth 12 marks and part (b) 24 marks then you would be expected to write twice as much for part (b) as part (a).

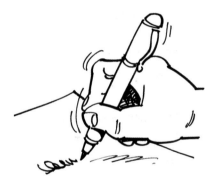

Timing:
Pay attention to the timing of your answer. If part (a) carries a lower mark allocation then you should spend less time answering it than part (b). A frequent error among candidates is that they spend roughly the same amount of time on each section and, on occasions, actually spend longer on part (a) than part (b). This will not score you high marks!

Command words:
Spend time looking at what each sub-question is asking you to do, taking particular note of the command words. If the question starts with 'To what extent …' then you need to make sure your answer looks at the factor mentioned in some detail and then evaluates it against other factors not mentioned in the question, taking care to ensure that you conclude with a judgement. Remember that your answer needs to be supported with accurate factual detail.

Quality of Written Communication (QWC):
Your answer should be written in paragraphs, remembering that your answer will be assessed, in part, on the quality of your written communication, namely spelling, punctuation and grammar. At all costs you must avoid using sub-headings, bullet points or abbreviations and ensure that you follow the basic rules of essay writing – introduction, discussion, conclusion. This will be required for the part (b) section but not necessarily for part (a). As part (a) will often be a descriptive type answer you might just write it in one long paragraph thus avoiding the need for introduction, discussion and conclusion.

Answering the open-ended essay question

1. Plan your essay carefully
- Planning what you are going to say is essential;
- Make a list of the key points and work out the best order to put them in;
- Under exam conditions you will not have time to make a detailed plan but it is still vital that you make a brief list of the key issues that need to be discussed;
- Once you have made your list put a number alongside each point so that you can follow a logical path;
- A good plan will make a good essay; spending a few minutes to organise your thoughts will enable you to give a structure to your essay;
- Contrary to what many Sixth Formers think, making a plan is not a waste of time but an invaluable tool to provide essential structure;
- Remember the importance of timing – allocate yourself sufficient time to complete each section of the essay.

2. Make sure you understand what the question is asking
- What are the command words?
- What are the specific dates?
- If the question covers a time span with a start and end date, make sure that you cover the whole time period;
- Does the question refer to a specific aspect such as domestic, economic, political, social and cultural?

3. Make sure you only include information that is relevant to the question
- Do not just write everything you know about the topic;
- Make sure the information actually answers the question;
- Make sure the information is accurate;
- Avoid plagiarism; do not just copy out sections from a textbook – be selective and reword the information to suit the demands of the question;
- Make regular references back to the question, either at the start or end of each paragraph, this helps to demonstrate links.

4. Make sure your argument is logical and is well supported
- This is needed to demonstrate knowledge and understanding;
- Make sure you include a range of specific examples;
- Aim to give a good breadth of coverage – do not adopt a narrow keyhole approach by focusing on just one or two issues;
- If the question requires consideration of a counter view or interpretation, make sure you devote sufficient time to each side of the argument – your answer needs to be balanced;
- Make sure you show links to the question itself;
- Try to link paragraphs so that the argument flows;
- Avoid cutting and pasting paragraphs of detail from Internet sites such as Wikipedia. This information will need to be filtered; selecting only what is relevant and necessary to answer the question.

5. The quality of written communication (spelling, punctuation and grammar)
- Take time to read over your essay to check that it reads well;
- Avoid using bullet points and abbreviations;
- Do not use text language, write words out in full;
- You must write in full sentences and break up the text into paragraphs;
- Remember the importance of the essay structure – introduction, discussion and conclusion.

How are AS and A Level essays marked?

When the essay comes to be marked it is done using a level of response mark scheme. This will be divided into four, sometimes five, levels of response, each of which will have some generic statements to define the standards expected at a particular level. At each level the competency skills will increase in demand, as is reflected in the generic statements listed below. These statements would then be followed with examples of the type of factual material the candidate would be expected to include in the answer.

Generic marking scheme for AS and A Level essays

	AO1a Demonstrate your **historical knowledge and understanding**, and **communicate** it in a clear and effective manner	AO1b Demonstrate your understanding of the past through **explanation, analysis** and making **substantiated judgements**	AO2b Demonstrate your ability to analyse and evaluate how aspects of the past have been **interpreted and represented in different ways**
Level 1	• you provide limited historical knowledge and your account is descriptive and generalised • the material may not always be accurate or relevant • the quality of written communication is weak with little connection between sections of your work	• you understand the basic idea in the set question • the explanation you offer is unbalanced and poorly focused • there are few if any links made to the question	• you only attempt to discuss the interpretation by tending to agree or disagree with the statement in the set question • there is little support to back up your observation
Level 2	• you provide mainly general knowledge about the set topic • aspects of your account are generally relevant • you demonstrate a reasonable quality of written communication	• you are able to explain and show understanding of the set issue • you attempt to make some links to the question • you make an attempt to reach a judgement about the question but it is not fully supported or balanced	• you demonstrate the ability to discuss the interpretation offered • your discussion of the interpretation is valid and you make reference to alternative interpretations but you do not properly evaluate or explain these
Level 3	• you provide accurate knowledge about the set issue • your account is relevant • you demonstrate a good quality of written communication with well-constructed sentences and paragraphs	• you are able to discuss the set issue with a consistent attempt to explain • you make regular links to the question • a judgement emerges in your answer and considers a counter-argument to that presented in the question	• you are able to discuss the interpretation offered in the context of one or more alternative interpretations • you begin to consider the interpretation in terms of the development of the historical debate that has taken place • you make some attempt to explain why the interpretations have been formed
Level 4	• you provide detailed and accurate knowledge about the set issue • your account is coherent, lucid and well-constructed • your spelling will be accurate and grammatical rules will be consistently applied	• you provide a focused explanation • you make clear and sustained links to the question throughout the account • a clear judgement is seen, which is balanced, substantiated and sustained throughout the essay	• you are able to discuss the interpretation offered in the context of alternative interpretations • you are able to consider the validity of the interpretations in terms of the development of historiographical context • you can demonstrate an understanding of how and why the issue has been interpreted in different ways

The characteristics of a good essay:

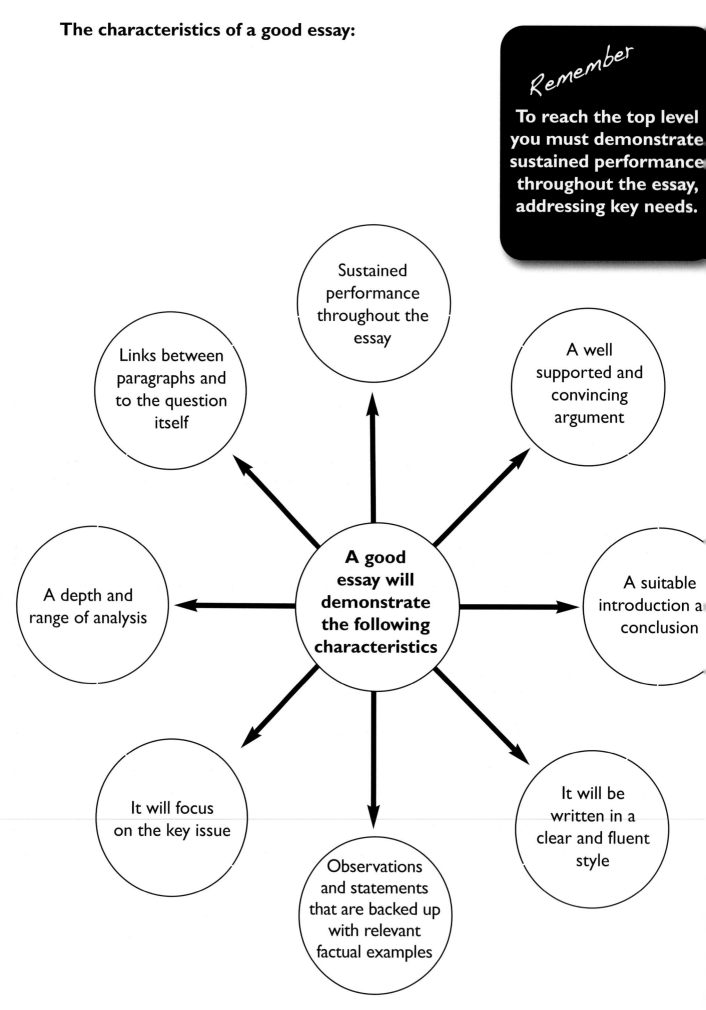

Remember

To reach the top level you must demonstrate sustained performance throughout the essay, addressing key needs.

Sustained performance throughout the essay

Links between paragraphs and to the question itself

A well supported and convincing argument

A good essay will demonstrate the following characteristics

A depth and range of analysis

A suitable introduction a conclusion

It will focus on the key issue

It will be written in a clear and fluent style

Observations and statements that are backed up with relevant factual examples

Having spent time looking at the theory behind the writing of a good essay, whether it be structured or open-ended, it is now time to look at a selection of essays written by AS and A Level candidates. One of the best ways of understanding what makes a good essay is to look at how others have attempted to answer a particular question, noting the strengths and weaknesses of their performances. You should assume that the following examples were written under timed conditions in an examination room, which will explain why some responses may seem to be a little brief and lacking in specific detail.

Examples of responses to the structured essay question

Key theme being tested: Life in Hitler's Germany, 1933-39.

Question:
1 (a) In what ways did educational policies reflect Nazi priorities in the years 1933-39?

  (b) How far was priority given to preparation for war in the economic policies of the Nazi regime?

Part (a) answers:

Advice and context on part (a) responses:

The key command words are '**In what ways did …**' which requires analysis of a key issue. In this case the focus of the question is the Nazi educational system and the degree to which its policies reflected Nazi priorities between the years 1933-39. The question requires you to identify Nazi priorities during these years such as:

- Securing the survival of the thousand year Reich through a process of indoctrinating young people in the ideals of National Socialism;
- The centralization of the school and university system;
- The control of the teaching staff and the reshaping of the curriculum to reflect Nazi ideology.

You could refer to such issues as:

- The drive for physical fitness;
- The importance of racial theory;
- The ideals of a master race;
- Some may see the Hitler Youth Movement as part of the educational drive to control youngsters and instil obedience and acceptance of Nazi ideology.

To reach the top level you will be expected to consider at least three issues, which will need to be supported with good factual detail. The answer will need to be coherent and analytical throughout, demonstrate connections between issues and attempt to prioritise. There will be a need for a reasoned conclusion or a good summative statement demonstrating a link back to the question itself.

Candidate A

(a) Nazi educational policies were aimed to indoctrinate the German youth. Teachers were told and forced only to teach how and what the Nazis wanted children to hear. Biology for example expressed the Nazi priority of a master race as it was used to display Aryan superiority. Physical education increased, increasing fitness for the Nazis next generation of soldiers. This can also suggest intentions of war. Jewish teachers were removed from school and eventually Jewish children.

> **Limited reference to education**

The Hitler Youth also educated children. It taught them how to fire a gun correctly, throw grenades and it had drills like the army; again this suggests making the male children soldiers. The girls in schools were taught how to knit, sow and how to spot the right man for a genetically 'pure' child. There was the league of German maidens that acted like the Hitler Youth training the girls to be healthy mothers, with similar drills to the Hitler Youth.

> **Brief reference to other factors but not developed**

In History, children were indoctrinated with great battles and the past failure and 'November criminals'. Geography taught the lands removed from Germany in the Treaty of Versailles and possible target countries for lebensraum.

> **Jumps back to curriculum**

The educational policies were used to create a generation of people that would support the Nazis without doubt and the increased PE suggested an army with which to fight.

The expelling of Jews which in slow succession led to genocide started with education as one of the first steps.

> **Lacks a conclusion or any direct links to the question**

Examiner's comments

Candidate A

The examiner felt that the candidate had tended to describe rather than analyse. There was little attempt to link the material to the question itself and the range of issues covered was rather narrow. Reference was made to some subjects taught and to the role of the Hitler Youth Movement. There was a brief reference to the importance of conformity but this theme was not developed. Overall the answer was relatively weak and lacked any attempt to prioritise or to reach a conclusion. It was awarded a Level Two mark.

Your task

What advice would you give Candidate A to improve the quality of their answer to enable it to receive a Level Four mark?

Candidate B

Spells out the importance of indoctrination

(a) There was a common saying of Jesuit priests once that if a child was brought up in their ways he would be theirs forever. Indoctrination of the young has been the goal of many ideologies aspiring to attain and maintain a dictatorship and Hitler and the Nazis beliefs were no exception.

Begins to discuss how education was used to indoctrinate

Propaganda was used very skilfully by Hitler and Goebbels and the educational system was adapted to further Nazi aims. Hitler's main goal was to achieve a 1000 year Reich and to do this he needed to impress obedience and reverence to authority into the next generation. Classrooms were filled with Nazi regalia such as a copy of Mein Kampf, swastikas and even a portrait of Hitler.

Begins to illustrate and expand the reference to indoctrination

The need to develop the Herrenvolk, the master race, was emphasised through the Nazi changes to the curriculum. In biology the theory of race was taught so as to make the children believe in the glorious destiny of Germany. History was taught from the Nazi point of view, which stressed that Germany had not been defeated in the Great War, only betrayed by Socialists, Communists and Jews. Literature, art and music were studied only to glorify great German achievement in those areas.

Moves on to show how ideology was put into practise

Sport was given extra emphasis in the new educational system, having 15% of the school day. This reflected Hitler's wish to have a strong healthy generation of Nazi warriors. Girls were taught homemaking skills and childcare reflecting Hitler's determination to raise the Aryan birth rate and his view of women as simply breeders of the next generation of men. Jewish children were banned from state schools and many Jewish university professors emigrated.

Demonstrates links back to the question and has a reasoned conclusion

As a result of the new educational policies educational standards diminished, but that was of little interest to the Nazis. Schools were seen as ways to instil the Nazis ideology into the next generation, to create a strong instinct of loyalty to Hitler and Nazi Germany, unquestioning obedience and a belief of the superiority of the Aryan race. Hitler acknowledged once that, despite his propaganda through the control of the media and mass rallies, there were many citizens who opposed his regime and the Nazi ideology, but he added 'their children are already ours'. This was the great priority of the Nazi state to ensure its survival, and through his new educational policies Hitler believed he had given birth to the next generation of the master race.

Examiner's comments

Candidate B

From the opening paragraph onwards the candidate has made a determined effort to focus upon the question and has analysed and debated the material. The examiner felt that this was a sophisticated answer, which commenced with an effective introduction that emphasised the importance of indoctrination, a key Nazi priority. The candidate covered a good range of issues, concentrating upon control of the curriculum, providing examples such as biology, history and physical education, but also examined the importance of indoctrination, showing how the two were intertwined. The answer was well developed, the line of argument was coherent, and the observations fully supported with relevant factual details. The conclusion was well reasoned and clearly addressed the thrust of the question. The answer was awarded a high Level Four mark.

Part (b) answers:

Advice and context on part (b) responses:

The command words in the question are '**How far** ...', which requires the candidate to reach a judgement and quantify the degree to which preparation for war dominated Nazi economic policies between 1933-39. If the candidate just describes economic policies after 1933, or accepts without due consideration to other factors that the economy was directed towards war production, then they will not advance far up the mark scheme. What is required is an analysis of the key economic policies, examining the factors that drove them. Better candidates will note a change in priority in 1936 following the 'Guns V Butter' debate, and the eventual resignation of Schacht over Hitler's demand for war production over consumerism. This led to Göring and the Four Year Plan initiative. The best candidates will note the interconnection between some of these priorities in the economy. To reach the higher levels there will need to be a debate, considering the evidence for and against the priority o war production, together with a clear judgement in relation to the actual question.

Candidate A

(b) After Adolf Hitler and the Nazis came to power, almost every aspect of Germany's economic policies were geared towards an eventual war. The army was increased, tanks and weapons were produced in a huge project of rearmament, autarky (Self-Sufficiency, the ability to function even during a war) initiatives were set in motion and plans to capture resources needed for war were drawn up and carried out.

A clear indication of how much priority was given to preparation for war can be seen through the 'guns butter' debate. After the unemployment crisis and economic status of Germany in the late 1920s/ear 1930s, Hitler was faced with a decision – did he continue his process of rearmament and put all of Germany's resources towards that (Guns), or did he slow down rearmament to allow the economy to stabilise and allow the German population consumer goods (Butter)? Hitler refused to slow rearmamer even going against the advice of Hjalmar Schacht, the Economic Minister and President of the Reichsbank, meaning that he was going to focus on guns rather than butter (consumer goods were restricted as Hitler did not want the country to rely on foreign imports). He put war before his people.

In 1936, Hitler announced the 4 Year Plan. This contained plans to have the armed forces ready for war within 4 years, and to have an economy able to support a war within 4 years. This was the clearest indication yet that Hitler was not going to let the economy consolidate as Schacht had advised, but that he was going to continue and even speed up the pace of rearmament. After the Treaty of Versailles, the German Army had been reduced to just 100,000 men, but by the late 1930s it had been increased to 1.4 million. By going against the Treaty of Versailles, Hitler made it clear that his priority was war.

As well as recruiting soldiers, the process of rearmament included producing all the necessary equipment needed for a war – weapons, tanks, submarines, aircraft. As it was just coming out of an economic crisis (1929 Wall Street Crash, 6 million unemployed in 1933), Germany couldn't afford to pa for these, so had to rely on Schacht to find a way around it. He did so by using Mefo Bills, which were basically I.O.U.'s given to the major companies and industries producing the war materials, saying they'll pay them when they can afford to. They also had the effect of keeping the amount of money spent on rearmament a secret so foreign powers wouldn't interfere.

Probably the largest German economic policy that showed the priority war was given was the autarky scheme. During a war, Germany wouldn't be able to cope if they relied too much on foreign imports, so Hitler wanted the country to become self sufficient. This meant spending vast amounts of money on developing synthetic oil and rubber, and mining German iron ore, even though it was of poor quality. The majority of German finance was aimed towards this, instead of directly benefiting the general populus.

After Adolf Hitler and the Nazis came to power in Germany in 1933, it would have made sense for them to have consolidated and secured their economy before embarking on massive, expensive projects. But Hitler's priority was to prepare Germany for war. If this meant spending millions of marks on strengthening the army and producing synthetic alternatives instead of allowing the German public simple consumer goods, then so be it.

Examiner's comments

The Examiner concluded that the focus on the question was generally good and the answer was supported with relevant factual detail, which demonstrated a reasonable understanding of this topic. However, there was some imbalance in the answer as it only dealt with the 'yes' side to the question, concentrating on how the economy was geared to war. There was no counter argument given, which would have lifted the answer to the top of Level Three or into Level Four. For this reason the range was considered to be limited, and both the introduction and conclusion only mentioned how the economy was geared to war. There needs to be more of a debate, considering the arguments over the 'Guns V Butter' dilemma in more depth. For these reasons the answer was awarded a mid-Level Three mark.

Candidate B

(b) The economic policies of the Nazis were to prepare for war which would be inevitable in acquiring living space in the east and defeating communist USSR. However, the economic policies also had to help the groups in German society who were important to Nazi ideology such as the peasantry and the Mittlestand.

The preparation for war was a huge issue which dominated the majority of Nazi economic policies. The dilema of guns vs butter arose as the country needed to increase rearmament for war, however there was a shortage of dairy goods and there was a demand for consumer goods. The Four Year Plan was introduced to prepare the economy for a potential war and work towards the Nazis goal of autarky. However Hitler was aware that his rise to power was partly due to the populations want for improvements in their living standards, and therefore total production of war weaponry could not be achieved as consumer goods had to be also produced to satisfy the population. Schacht's New Plan and Mefo bills were also used in the road to a war economy as well as trying to stabilize the balance of payments deficit.

The Nazis regime also gave the creation of jobs a priority as this was the basis of them winning power. They invested in businesses to create jobs and built the autobahns as a way of creating jobs, this was done by the method of labour intensive which although created more jobs, was not efficient. The creation of jobs did help the war preparations as many jobs that were created were in munitions factories and conscription into the army decreased unemployment and increased the size of the army.

The peasantry were seen as the backbone of the Nazi society and the Nazis embarked on a policy of 'Blood and Soil'. This included economic policies which were to increase the economic status of the peasantry and their work and living conditions. The Reich Food Estate set wages, production quotas and crop rotation in an attempt to attract the population back to the countryside. The Reich Farm Entailed Law meant that farms of around 30 acres could not be split up but were to be inherited by the eldest son. However Nazi government intervention failed the peasantry as by 1939 there were labour shortages, a decrease of 20% in productivity, peasants living standards were lower and their economic status had declined.

The Mittlestand were the Nazis most loyal supporters and they were given help by the regime to survive against the threat of department stores. They were given preferential treatment by state agencies, competition was curbed and from 1933 the establishment of new department stores was banned. However Nazi ideology conflicted with their aims as big businesses were more efficient in the build up to war and were able to invest more in research and development. The Mittlestand were abandoned by the Nazi regime in favour of big businesses and were stuck between price freezes in the shops and out priced by the Reich Food Estate.

In conclusion the Nazi ideology and their aims conflicted; the regime gave high priorities to the groups such as the peasantry and Mittlestand who were favoured due to ideology, however the reality of their aims won. A massive priority was given to preparation for war. Ultimately the Nazis were willing to abandon their loyal supporters in favour for large businesses. Their policy of creating jobs for the 6 million who were unemployed at the beginning of the regime was very important, and it did contribute to the economy when preparing for war, despite the economic inefficiency of labour intensive jobs.

Examiner's comments

The examiner felt that the candidate had not developed their answer in any depth and the enquiry was both narrow focused and lacking in depth of analysis and evaluation. There was a tendency for the candidate to 'tell the story' in places, concentrating too much on the narrative. While there was reference to 'Guns V Butter' the issue was not discussed in any detail and there was little mention of the policies of Schacht in the period 1933-36 or Göring's Four Year Plan after this date. While there was an attempt to reach a judgement the analysis was superficial. For this reason the answer was awarded a low Level Three mark.

Your task

Explain why both candidates did not reach Level Four in the mark scheme. What was missing from their answers?

Examples of responses to the open-ended essay question

Question: To what extent was the German invasion of Belgium in 1914 mainly responsible for Britain's involvement in the First World War?

Advice and context

What is the examiner looking for?

The key command word in the question is '**To what extent …**' and the candidate would be expected to evaluate the importance of the given factor against a range of other factors. In this instance the violation of Belgian neutrality by Germany has been identified in the question as the main reason for Britain's entry into the war. The candidate would be expected to evaluate how important Britain's promise of 1839 to protect Belgian neutrality was in her decision to go to war in 1914. This factor would then need to be weighed up alongside a range of other factors such as:

- Britain's growing rapprochement with Russia and France;
- Her naval and colonial antagonism with Germany;
- Her military and naval connections with France;
- Britain's concerns over the Balance of Power;
- The ambiguity of Sir Edward Grey's foreign policy.

The specific crises of 1906, 1911 and 1912/13 could be examined to provide context.

To achieve Level Four, the top level, in the mark scheme the answer will need to demonstrate a coherent argument and a consistent evaluative approach that focuses directly on the question. In the introduction the candidate will have identified the range of factors that will be considered in the essay, and in the conclusion these will have been ranked in importance and a final judgement given as to whether the attack on Belgium was the main reason for Britain entering the war.

Candidate C

The German invasion of Belgium in 1914 was a major factor in Britain's decision to join in the First World War.

Questions can be raised as to whether it was the main reason. Britain was part of an Entente with France and although this did not commit Britain to Frances defence, France believed that in the event of war Britain would come to her aid. She was also bound by her secret naval agreement with France that, again, was not a solid commitment but it led France to believe in British support.

The naval race with Germany was unquestionably another factor. Britain had always had the best navy and, despite much opposition from other British politicians, they built a 'Super' ship called a Dreadnought to continue this achievement. However, Germany responded and built a bigger navy and more 'Dreadnoughts'. Britain saw this as a direct threat as Germany did not need a navy to invade any other European country. At the start of the 1900s Britain thought of Germany as the most likely country to have a natural alliance with. As a result Germany's rising aggression came as a shock to Britain, who right up until 1914 never stopped trying to form a political agreement with Germany that could prevent a war.

Britain throughout this entire time of foreign policy has tried to maintain the Balance of Power, this is a fundamental reason behind her decision to back France. Belgium was a small country who was supposed to remain neutral at all costs. When Germany broke this rule it pushed Britain into the war but it was not the biggest factor. The reason given for the war by Salisbury was that Britain felt she had no choice. She needed to keep good relations with France and Russia and she wanted to maintain the Balance of Power. German expansionism could not be allowed.

During the Moroccan crisis Germany had caused trouble for Britain, after that she and France agreed to an alliance over Morocco. Germany attempted to break it up by telling the Moroccan Sultan that Germany would back their independence. Although this ultimately brought Britain and France closer, this was the second time that Germany had crossed Britain's interests. The first was during the Boer War, more specifically, the Kruger Telegram. Britain had invited Germany to watch her battle against the Boers. Germany saw the skills of the Boer fighters and offered her services. These were both very minor factors in Britain's decision for war but they did contribute to Britain's feelings for Germany changing.

After Britain came out of Splendid Isolation and started making alliances and ententes with France and Russia, Germany felt trapped and fought back. In a bid to avoid conflict Britain tried to come to an agreement with Germany. All she would have Britain do was join her. However Britain could see that Germany would lose and she could not afford to back her and risk losing all good relations with Europe and being forced back into a position of isolation.

In conclusion, Britain had many major reasons for her involvement in the First World War. Germany's invasion of Belgium was merely the push she needed to make the final, crucial decision. It was the fear of isolation, the unspoken promise to France and her fear of Germany's threat against the Balance of Power that fuelled Britain's campaign to go to war.

Examiner's comments

The candidate did not actually deal with the main issue – the violation of Belgian neutrality – in any detail. A number of other factors were identified but these were not evaluated or discussed in any great detail. Factual detail was patchy, with a few historical inaccuracies in places. Both the introduction and conclusion were weak and there were few links made to connect paragraphs or to demonstrate coherence of argument. The structure of the essay was considered to be unbalanced and was given a mark at the top of Level Two.

Candidate D

The German invasion of Belgium in 1914 was partly responsible for British involvement in the First World War because it could be seen as breaking the Treaty of London of 1839 and therefore jeopardising and not respecting Belgium independence and neutrality. However, it is most likely that this event was the final event that sparked war after a long deterioration of British-German relations.

Before 1900 a possible future British-German alliance looked a likely possibility, with British ministers describing Germany as a 'natural ally' because of cultural and economic similarities. However, in the latter part of the nineteenth century the relationship between Britain and Germany began to deteriorate with the conflict over the Kruger Telegram in 1896. The Jameson Raid involving the Vitlanders in 1895, a revolt for an increase in political rights for Vitlanders, which was heavily suppressed by Boer troops led to the Kruger Telegram of 1896, where the Kaiser congratulated Kruger for putting down the revolt. The British ministers were extremely annoyed by this unprovoked attack by Germany and support of the Boers. This started the deterioration in British and German relations which culminated in the expectation of war with Germany. Even Grey saw it an inevitable.

The Arms Race, started by Britain building the first Dreadnought in 1906 further soured relations with Germany as Britain's navy was seen as essential to the defence of Britain, while Germany's was not, theirs was almost just a show of wealth and power. The 'Naval Holiday' proposed by Britain in 1913 was bitterly refused by Germany which further soured relations.

Furthermore, the French Entente was seen as anti-German because there was no perceived threat from the French. The terms discussed proposed that the French navy would help patrol waters that the British already patrolled, leading to a reduction of pressure on the British navy. This allowed Britain to just position her navy in home waters (eg. the Channel) which showed a perceived threat from Germany. (Britain's navy had been further reduced from its over-stretched position previously by the Anglo-Japanese Treaty of 1902).

The Entente brought France and Britain closer and led to military talks with a hypothetical enemy, Germany. This showed the extent to which a threat from Germany and war was considered likely or inevitable.

Lloyd George's Mansion House speech of 1911 was considered anti-German as it gave the impression that Britain would support France if the chance arose of war. With the deterioration of Anglo-German relations Britain saw war as inevitable and psychological results proved that after a long period of peace in a country the people look forward to war.

The Anglo-Russian Entente of 1907 saw France, Russia and Britain draw into a triple Entente and deprived Russia of a potential ally. This also split Europe into two, The Triple Alliance and Triple Entente.

Britain could also be seen as entering the war to remain loyal to the French Entente. Britain had just moved out of a period of isolation prior to 1900 and therefore if she failed to support the French who were threatened by Germany she would be seen as unreliable and would not be trusted for future alliances.

British foreign policy further gave reason to Britain's involvement in the First World War. The 'Balance of Power' was a key factor in Britain's view of the European powers and by Germany becoming increasingly dominant in European relations she needed to be suppressed. Diplomatic means of doing this had failed which meant that the last resort was war, which Britain intended to go into if it meant a return to the 'Balance of Power'.

Therefore the German invasion of Belgium in 1914 was the final event which contributed to a mass of events between Britain and Germany which led to World War One. However, just as important reasons for entering the First World War were maintaining the traditional British foreign policy of the 'Balance of Power' and the deterioration of Anglo-German relations and the Naval Race which

Germany had no intention of ceasing and which could have been interpreted as preparation for war on Britain. Germany, surrounded by land countries was definitely not preparing for a land war by building Dreadnoughts, therefore the only perceived threat is from the sea, i.e. preparation for war with Britain. Finally, Britain had to remain loyal to her Entente with France, and with the knowledge that France and Russia would support her (due to the Triple Entente) she could enter into the war in the knowledge that she'd not be 'going it alone'.

Examiner's comments

The candidate considered the key issue – Britain's commitment to protect Belgian neutrality – and evaluated its importance in Britain's decision to go to war alongside a range of other factors. The candidate demonstrated a good depth of knowledge and understanding of the topic and constructed a reasoned and well-supported argument. There were regular links back to the question, with judgments being made as to the relative importance of factors in Britain's decision making. There were also links made between paragraphs thus demonstrating a coherence of argument. The examiner felt that the essay was a little short on references to the involvement of Sir Edward Grey and to the concept of the Balance of Power, hence it was awarded a mark at the lower end of Level Four.

Your task

Looking through the essay of both Candidates C and D consider the following:

1. Identify the section of the essay dealing with the issue of Belgian neutrality.

2. What other factors does the candidate consider?

3. Examine the introduction and conclusion. Are they reasoned? Does the introduction set the scene and the conclusion sum up the argument and reach a judgement?

4. Underline the sentences that show a link to the essay question.

5. How do the two essays differ in terms of style and writing technique? Have they attempted to consider the key issue – To what extent …?

6. Do you think the examiner has been fair in the awarding of the marks?

SUMMARY OF CHAPTER TWO

Having studied Chapter Two you should now have a better understanding of:
- The different styles of essay questions asked at AS and A Level;
- The importance and purpose of command words in the essay question;
- How to structure your essay in response to these command words;
- How your essay will be marked and what the examiner will be looking for in a good essay;
- A level of response mark scheme and what you need to do to score the highest level of response.

You should also have:

- Marked examples of candidate responses and have an understanding of why they scored the marks they did, noting both their strengths and weaknesses;
- Received advice and tips on how to write good essays.

Your task is now to take heed of these comments and write first class essays of your own.

CHAPTER THREE

DEMONSTRATING THE SKILLS OF THE HISTORIAN

Analysing and evaluating historical sources

Historians operate like detectives. They search for clues or evidence that the past has left behind. They have to interpret the evidence they find and make reasoned judgements with regards to its relevance and reliability.

The majority of the evidence available to historians comes in the form of written sources. These sources need to go through a rigorous process of analysis and evaluation if their true value is to be ascertained.

An essential part of the study of History is the evaluation of source material, and the nurturing of the skills required to undertake this forms a key component of both the AS and A Level course.

Assessment Objective 2(a) demands that as part of an historical enquiry AS and A Level candidates demonstrate the skill of:

'analysing and evaluating a range of appropriate source material with discrimination.'

You will have dealt with sources at GCSE but you are now required to examine them in a more sophisticated fashion, demonstrating a more advanced level of analysis and evaluation. The examiner is attempting to find out how well you can handle selective evidence, relate it to what you know about the period under study and make a reasoned judgement as to its usefulness, accuracy and reliability as a piece of historical evidence.

When analysing and evaluating a piece of evidence you will be expected to perform a range of specific tasks, demonstrating your ability to:

- Undertake the **comprehension** of the **content** of the source;
- Put the source into its **historical context**, relating it to the **bigger picture**;
- Make a **judgement** about the **validity** of the source;
- Make a **judgement** about the **usefulness** of the source;
- Make a **judgement** about the **reliability** of the source;
- **Compare** and **contrast** sources;
- **Consider different interpretations** when comparing sources, and suggest **why the viewpoints may differ**;
- Comment upon **how the author reached this judgement.**

Different types of sources are available to the historian

(a)   Written sources

Written sources are many and varied and can include such items as a letter, a diary, a memoir, an autobiography, a speech, a newspaper and the writings of historians.

All written sources can by divided into two camps – evidence that comes from the time that you are studying and evidence that was produced after these events have taken place. Historians traditionally refer to evidence that is concurrent with the event being studied as **contemporary evidence**, while all that is written afterwards is considered to be **reflective evidence** composed with the benefit of hindsight. Such differing types of evidence are often given the labels of **primary** and **secondary** evidence, although these labels can sometimes be misleading and lead to problems of interpretation.

THE DIFFERENCE BETWEEN CONTEMPORARY AND REFLECTIVE ACCOUNTS

Contemporary viewpoints [E.g. Eye-witness accounts]	Accounts written with the benefit of reflection and hindsight [E.g. Accounts produced by historians]
• Contemporary evidence is the raw material of the historian; • It is evidence produced at the time that the events described in the source took place; • Contemporary evidence could be physical remains of the past such as ruins, pottery and weapons or eye-witness accounts of what went on such as written and visual material. *Example of contemporary evidence:* *The diary of Anne Frank* 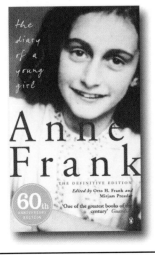	• It is evidence that does not come from the time being studied but from a later period; • It is usually the work of historians who have written about the past; • It is their interpretation of the events based upon their analysis of the sources they have studied; • These reflections provide interpretations of contemporary sources. *Example of reflective evidence:* *A book about the holocaust* 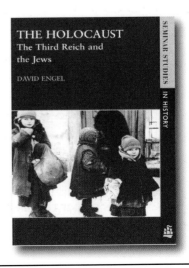

When historians write about the past they use a combination of contemporary sources and later reflections to reach their own interpretation of events. The biography of the eighteenth century Prime Minister William Pitt the Younger, for example, which was written by William Hague, is a reflection by a modern historian since it was published in 2004 and is the viewpoint obtained with the benefit of hindsight. Hague was not alive at the time of William Pitt and he is writing over two centuries after his death. However, Hague could not have written his detailed study without consulting a range of contemporary evidence such as the transcripts of Pitt's speeches to the House of Commons, letters between Pitt and his contemporaries, excerpts from the diaries and journals of fellow MPs, the memoirs of those who knew Pitt, together with reports found in the newspapers of the time. Some of this contemporary material would have been quoted in the biography, to which Hague would have added his own commentary and reflection.

An example of how historians interpret and record the past: an excerpt taken from Hague's biography of William Pitt.

The historian's interpretation and reflection →

Contemporary evidence →

'Shortly after Pitt became Prime Minister, Wraxall wrote his famous account of his personal style:

… in his manners, Pitt, if not repulsive, was cold, stiff, and without suavity or amenity. He seemed never to invite approach or to encourage acquaintance, though when addressed he could be polite, communicative, and occasionally gracious … From the instant that Pitt entered the doorway of the House of Commons, he advanced up the floor with a quick and firm step, his head erect and thrown back, looking neither to the right nor to the left, nor favouring with a nod or a glance any of the individuals seated on either side, among whom many who possessed five thousand pounds a year would have been gratified even by so slight a mark of attention. It was not thus that Lord North or Fox treated Parliament, nor from them would Parliament have so patiently endured it; but Pitt seemed made to guide and to command, even more than to persuade or to convince, the assembly that he addressed.

The historian's interpretation and reflection →

His immense intellectual self-confidence was combined with a second factor: the expectation that his hour would come. In part this was the natural feeling of a young man who had advanced far in politics at an early age.'
© 2004, William Hague

A contemporary portrait of Pitt →

In this example Hague has quoted from a contemporary of Pitt, a man who observed how he acted in the House of Commons and who was familiar with his personality and demeanour. This is contemporary evidence and linked to it Hague has added his own interpretation of Pitt's self-confidence. This illustrates the process of reflection that epitomises the work of the historian.

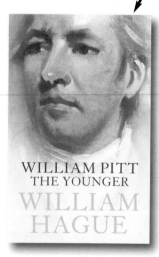

WILLIAM PITT
THE YOUNGER
WILLIAM
HAGUE

An important source of published contemporary evidence for historians is the press. Newspapers are valuable historical documents since they provide a day-to-day record of events and reflect the political and social views that had the most impact at that time. An example of their value can be gleaned through the work of Thomas Campbell Foster, a reporter for *The Times*, who was sent down to southwest Wales from London to report upon the disturbances caused by the Rebecca rioters in 1843. Writing for *The Times* you would expect Campbell Foster to be a supporter of the establishment and consequently to be critical of the rural protests taking place in Carmarthenshire and Pembrokeshire. This was not the case and his reports demonstrate some compassion for the plight of the farmers, as the following extract demonstrates:

'The main cause of the mischief is beyond doubt the poverty of the farmers. They have become thereby discontented at every tax and burden they have been called upon to pay. If to this … can be added an unjust imposition [the tolls] you have the crowning climax, however trivial it may appear in itself, which has fanned this discontent into a flame.'

Thomas Campbell Foster reporting in *The Times*, 26 June 1843

Campbell Foster's investigative reports into the events of 1843-44 in southwest Wales have provided historians with a valuable source of primary evidence relating to the Rebecca riots. Campbell Foster was there when these events took place, he was a contemporary who interviewed people involved in them and he was able to reach judgements concerning the causes of the disturbances. It is the job of the historian to evaluate the reliability and importance of his reporting.

The difficulties of determining whether a source is a contemporary viewpoint or a later reflection

It is not always easy to determine whether a piece of evidence is a contemporary viewpoint or a later reflection, and this can impact upon its usefulness to the historian. Should the Bayeux Tapestry, for instance, be regarded as a contemporary viewpoint or a later reflection? The tapestry is treated as a record of the events surrounding the Battle of Hastings in 1066. It is contemporary evidence in terms of the sorts of wools used to make the tapestry, the dyes used to obtain the colours and of the techniques of the needlewomen. It is also a contemporary view of what the Normans wanted the world to know about the battle. However, it is not a contemporary view of the battle itself but a later reflection, composed with some element of hindsight. It was commissioned after the battle and the women who carried out the needlework were not present on the battlefield at Hastings. It is not known how they obtained details of the actual sequence of events of 14th October 1066. We must presume that they obtained such details from oral testimony. In this sense the tapestry is a later reflection rather than a contemporary account.

Your task

This task is based upon the events of the sinking of the passenger liner the *Lusitania* in May 1915 and will involve you in making evaluations and judgements about the usefulness and reliability of a range of historical sources.

Context: the *Lusitania* was on the final stage of its voyage across the Atlantic from New York to Liverpool. It was sunk off the coast of southern Ireland by a single torpedo fired from the German submarine U-20. The ship sank in just 18 minutes with the loss of 1,201 lives. The tragedy occurred in mid-afternoon on 7 May 1915 during the first year of the Great War. The German authorities claimed that the passenger liner was a legitimate target for attack as it was carrying weapons of war but both the British and American authorities denied this.

Study each of the sources A–E and then answer the questions that follow.

Source A

The front page of the *New York Times* newspaper that was published the day after the sinking of the *Lusitania*.

Source B

A representation in the form of a painting showing the sinking of the *Lusitania*. The artist was not present to witness the actual event.

Source C

An illustration of the wreck of the *Lusitania* sitting on the seabed with a large hole in the hull caused by the torpedo. The image was created by the artist Ken Marschall using information obtained from Dr. Robert Ballard's exploration of the wreck site by submarine in 1993.

Painting by Ken Marschall ©1994

Source D

A still from a BBC drama-documentary called *The sinking of the Lusitania*, which was first shown on TV in 2008. The scene shows passengers trying to escape the sinking ocean liner.

Source E

'3.10 pm.   Clear bow shot at 700 m… angle of intersection 90 [degrees] estimated speed 22 nautical miles.

Shot struck starboard side close behind the bridge. An extraordinary heavy detonation followed, with a very large cloud of smoke (far above the front funnel). A second explosion must have followed that of the torpedo (boiler or coal or powder?).

The superstructure above the point of impact and the bridge were torn apart; fire broke out; light smoke veiled the high bridge. The ship stopped immediately and quickly listed sharply to starboard, sinking deeper by the head at the same time.

Great confusion arose on the ship; some of the boats were swung clear and lowered into the water. Many people must have lost their lives; several boats loaded with people rushed downward, struck the water bow or stern first and filled at once.

On the port side, because of the sloping position, fewer boats were swung clear than on the starboard side.'

Extract from the diary of Walter Schwieger, captain of the German submarine U-20.
He fired a single torpedo at the *Lusitania* at 3.10 pm on 7 May 1915. It hit its target amidships.

Your task

1. Examine each of the five sources and determine whether you would class each individual source as either a contemporary or a reflective piece of evidence. Give full reasons for your decision.

2. Which of the sources would you consider to be most useful to the historian attempting to uncover the actual events surrounding the sinking of the ocean liner?

3. Which of the sources would your consider to be most reliable as pieces of evidence? Give full reasons for your answer.

Are later reflections of more use to the historian than contemporary accounts?

A common misconception by history students is that contemporary sources are of little use because they are biased in their opinion. However, this is not the case as not all contemporary evidence is biased and even if it is, it can still be useful because it gives us information on how people were thinking at that time. Part of the task of the historian is to consider why and how they came to hold that particular viewpoint. Conversely, it follows that not all later reflections by historians are balanced and unbiased. They may well have been writing with the benefit of hindsight but their interpretation of events could be representative of a particular viewpoint they hold because of particular political, religious or cultural issues that are important to them. The balance of their interpretation will also depend upon what contemporary sources and works of other historians they have consulted during their investigation. Marxist historians, for instance, will tend to emphasise the class struggle in their interpretation of the causes of such events as the English Civil War and the French Revolution. It is therefore important that you, as an A Level student, pay particular attention to the credentials and authority of the author of the source as this can impact upon their interpretation.

In this context a later reflection can be no more useful to an historian than a contemporary account. Both have their merits and their weaknesses.

(b)   Visual sources

Visual evidence can take many forms. For example, it could be a photograph, a cartoon, a painting, a drawing, a map or statistical data. Each of these will have their uses to the historian.

(i) Photographs

Photographs can be extremely useful to the historian but, like all types of evidence, they must be treated with care and be subjected to a rigorous process of analysis and evaluation. When examining photographs:

- It is important to consider the context in which the photograph was taken;

- Bear in mind that most photographers would carefully select the best viewpoints for their photographs if they could;

- It is important to realise that the camera can lie and photographs are sometimes deliberately altered to suit a particular need;

- Some photographs have been deliberately faked.

Source A

This photograph may appear useful to an historian as it shows Lenin and Stalin deep in conversation in Gorki, an area of Moscow, in 1922. It gives the impression that the two men are friends but the photograph is actually a fake produced in the late 1920s for the purpose of boosting Stalin's status and importance in the power struggle that emerged to replace Lenin. In the original photograph Lenin is sitting by himself.

Source B

This photograph shows the war recruiting office at Southwark Town Hall in London in December 1915. The men appear to be very jovial and enthused. They have been asked by the photographer to hold this pose while he takes the picture. Images such at these formed part of the propaganda campaign designed to help encourage men to join up for the war and emphasised the importance of patriotic duty. For this source to be useful to the historian it is important to understand the **context** in which it was produced.

Your task

1. Source A is a faked photograph produced in the early 1920s. Explain why it could be useful to an historian studying Stalin's rise to power.

2. Would Source B be of any use to an historian studying the methods used by the British Government to encourage recruitment during the early stages of the war? Explain your answer fully.

In order to analyse and evaluate a photograph in depth it is necessary to subject it to a series of probing questions:

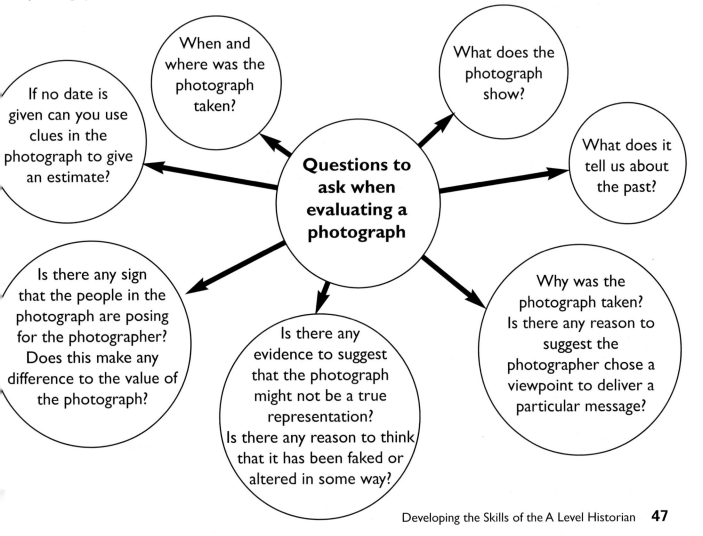

(ii) Cartoons

It is quite common for a question on an AS or A Level examination paper to demand the evaluation of a cartoon as a piece of historical evidence. The cartoon provides a particular interpretation of an event and it is your task to identify, explain and demonstrate an understanding of that interpretation. A good starting point is to annotate the cartoon by identifying the key figures and features, comment upon the significance and meaning of any labels or writing, try to explain the meaning of any caption, and try to pick out the main message of the cartoon. Ask yourself what the cartoonist is trying to say, what standpoint the cartoonist is taking, and whether the cartoon confirms or contradicts your understanding of the event in question. The following is an example of how a cartoon might be annotated:

The SA raise both hands in submission to Hitler's authority. Contrast this to the usual one arm Nazi salute.

Göring is depicted as Thor, the God of War, the blood signifying that he played a part in the killings.

The German army who are now going to take control of the SA.

Hitler has double crossed the SA. They have helped him into power and he has now turned against them.

Goebbels peers between Hitler's legs, being a minor figure in this event.

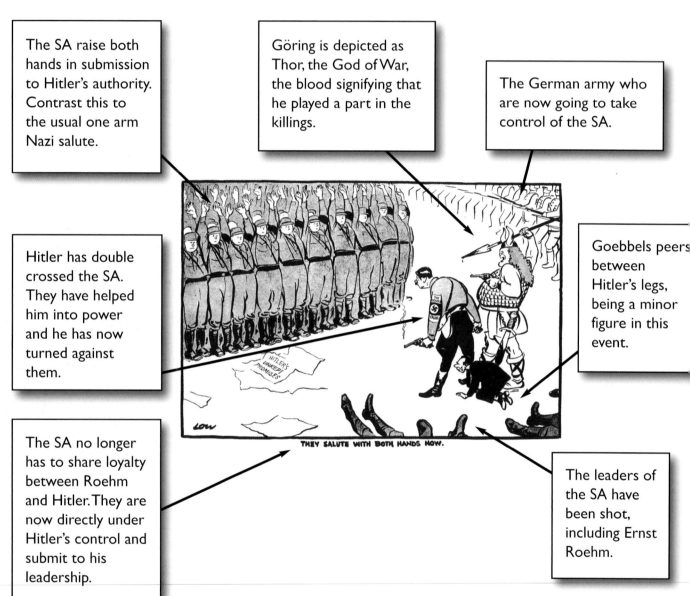

The SA no longer has to share loyalty between Roehm and Hitler. They are now directly under Hitler's control and submit to his leadership.

The leaders of the SA have been shot, including Ernst Roehm.

A cartoon by David Low depicting the Night of the Long knives, 30 June 1934.
It was published in a British newspaper *The Evening Standard* on 3 July 1934.
British Cartoon Archive, University of Kent.

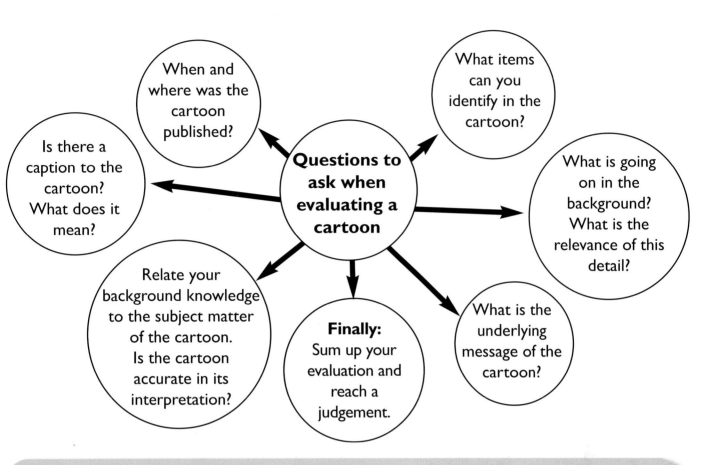

When and where was the cartoon published?

What items can you identify in the cartoon?

Is there a caption to the cartoon? What does it mean?

Questions to ask when evaluating a cartoon

What is going on in the background? What is the relevance of this detail?

Relate your background knowledge to the subject matter of the cartoon. Is the cartoon accurate in its interpretation?

Finally: Sum up your evaluation and reach a judgement.

What is the underlying message of the cartoon?

Your task

Apply the evaluation questions listed in the diagram above to this cartoon.

Questions:

(a) What information about the Rebecca riots can you glean from this cartoon?

(b) How reliable would this source be to an historian studying the Rebecca riots?

REBECCA AND HER DAUGHTERS.

Tolltaker . . Sɪʀ R. P—ʟ.   Irish Rebecca . D—ʟ O'C—ʟ.   *Rebecca's Daughters* by Mᴇᴍʙᴇʀs ᴏғ ᴛʜᴇ Rᴇᴘᴇᴀʟ Ass— ɴ.

A contemporary cartoon showing Rebecca rioters attacking a tollgate. The image appeared in 1843 in *Punch*, a magazine aimed at the middle classes.

(iii) Paintings and illustrations

As with cartoons, paintings and illustrations can be useful pieces of historical evidence, but they need to be treated with care and subjected to the same process of evaluation. Both paintings and illustrations are not exact visual images but are representations of events by artists and, as a consequence, their accuracy needs to be considered with care when evaluating their usefulness and reliability. An oil painting by Charles Cundall, for example, which depicts the evacuation of British troops from the beaches of Dunkirk in May/June 1940, is often reproduced in history textbooks to illustrate the evacuation process. Yet its value as an historical source is open to question.

The evacuation from Dunkirk during May/June 1940. A contemporary oil painting by Charles Cundall who was sent by the British government to produce an official painting of events on the beaches of Dunkirk.

Charles Cundall was commissioned by the British government to paint an official representation of the evacuation and was sent to the beaches of Dunkirk. He presumably made sketches of the scenes he witnessed and took photographs. He would have supplemented this with additional research, which would have involved studying photographs taken by others at the time and evaluating the oral testimony of some of the evacuated troops and also the sailors involved. His painting, which was finished during the war, is therefore his interpretation of the evacuation at Dunkirk, based upon his own research and his understanding of the evidence that he uncovered.

Your task

1. Do you consider the painting by Charles Cundall showing the evacuation of British forces from Dunkirk in May/June 1940 to be a contemporary source or a later reflection? Give full reasons for your answer.

2. How would you test the accuracy of Cundall's representation of the events at Dunkirk?

(c)   Oral history

Oral history is spoken history. It is peoples' memories or recollections of the past told to historians rather than written down as memoirs. Celebrated TV documentaries such as *The World at War* produced in the 1970s and *The Peoples' Century* produced in the 1990s have made extensive use of the oral testimony of people who lived through the events under investigation. There is a tendency among students to dismiss oral evidence, concluding that it cannot be relied upon because it is based upon memory and therefore it will not be exact. However, with careful consideration of possible distortion and accuracy, it can prove a useful tool to historians. In many respects it is no different from a story in a newspaper that was compiled from interviews obtained by the reporter, the only significant difference being the time lapse.

When using oral history as evidence historians have to consider potential weaknesses:

*   It can be inaccurate and unreliable as evidence;

*   It depends on human memory;

*   Memory is often selective;

*   Memory can be fallible and can distort.

Older people, for example, tend to remember the very good times or the very bad times, the ordinary times tend to be forgotten. They tend to make sweeping generalisations, often referring to the 'good old days'. In the lower school you may have been given the task of interviewing an elderly relative, asking them to recall their lives during the Second World War. They would have mentioned the hardship that existed on the Home Front, dwelling on such issues as rationing, evacuation and the black out, but the chances are that they would have said little about the more mundane day-to-day activities. They may remember some humorous stories or some sad tales as these are easiest to remember because they are out of the ordinary.

Think back to your time in primary school. The chances are you will remember things that have made a dramatic impact on your memory – an event that made you feel proud or conversely an incident you would want to forget but cannot because it was so bad. You will probably find it difficult to recall the ordinary and routine procedures of everyday school life. You remember the highs and lows and tend to forget the middle bits!

Oral history must therefore be treated with the same rigour as any other historical source. It may be unreliable but this does not make it useless:

- Oral sources can be cross-checked with other sources to determine accuracy;
- They reflect what people felt about events in the past;
- They show how events have been remembered.

(d)   Historical fiction

Fiction is deemed to be anything that has been invented or made up, such as stories, plays, novels and poems. Historical fiction writing is often based on fact. The authors have had to research the time period in order to make the story seem authentic. Recent novels such as *Birdsong* and *Private Peaceful* both of which recount conditions in the trenches in Flanders during the First World War, together with *The Boy in the Striped Pyjamas,* which deals with the ill-treatment of the Jews by the Nazis, owe part of their success to the fact that they provide a feel for a particular period and the attention to detail within them enables the reader to gain an appreciation of that period in time. For historical fiction to be successful it has to engage the reader and give the impression that it is a true representation of those times in the way that the novels of Charles Dickens helped to create an image of the hardship of life in the urban slums of Victorian London, or the writings of Thomas Hardy provided a visual image of life in a rural landscape during the same period. Such works can prove useful to students in helping to provide context to the understanding of particular periods of time but such works should not be treated as factual reports. Nor can they claim to be an accurate reflection of life at that time. When examining such material it should always be borne in mind that the aim of the novel is to entertain rather than to educate. Exaggeration and historical inaccuracies can be used to enhance the plot of a story and this must be taken into account when assessing usefulness and reliability.

The novels of Daniel Owen of Mold in Flintshire

Born in Mold in 1836 Daniel Owen was the youngest of seven children. When he was only a few months old his father and two of his brothers lost their lives when the Argoed coal mine in which they were working was flooded. Brought up in poverty Daniel received little schooling and at the age of twelve was apprenticed with a tailor in the town of Mold. Working in a shop meant that he was constantly meeting local people and this experience, together with his work as a non-conformist preacher, provided him with the background detail he needed when he came to write his novels.

A portrait of Daniel Owen painted towards the end of his life.

His various novels, written in Welsh but later translated into English, describe the lives of ordinary people, mostly based upon the people he knew in and around the town of Mold. His most important novel is considered to be *Rhys Lewis*, which appeared in 1885. It is an autobiography of Rhys whose hard life revolves around a host of tragedies which impinge upon himself and the community. The backdrop to the whole story are the events of the Mold Riots of 1869 when miners from Leeswood Green colliery clashed with troops sent to end the disturbances, the result being the death of four people during the fighting. In the novel Leeswood Green colliery is referred to as 'Y Caeau Cochion' and the works manager as 'Mr Strangle'. Other novels by Daniel Owen include *Enoc Huws* (1891), which tells the story of an illegitimate child reared in a workhouse who becomes a prosperous grocer and his subsequent troubles, and *Gwen Tomos* (1894), which depicts the emergence of Calvinistic Methodism in rural Flintshire in the second half of the eighteenth century. Daniel Owen died in 1895.

The Secret Room, a novel by Marion Eames, published in 1975.

The story, originally published in Welsh in 1969, is set in the reign of Charles II and follows the experiences of Rowland Ellis. He becomes a Quaker as a result of a neighbour but his wife does not share his beliefs. Following her death Ellis marries a sympathetic cousin. His religious persuasion is later betrayed to the authorities by a servant he has dismissed, who described a 'secret room' he claimed to have seen in the house containing objects of Catholic worship. Ellis and his fellow Quakers were arrested, imprisoned and illegally condemned to death. They were only saved by the direct intervention of the king. Following this religious persecution they decide to leave Wales for America and Ellis goes on to found a Welsh colony in Pennsylvania. The novel provides a vivid backdrop to the religious strife of the seventeenth century within the Welsh context.

For discussion:
Are the novels of such authors as Daniel Owen and Marion Eames of any use to the historian?

(e)   Internet sources

The latest and fastest growing depository of source material for students of history is the Internet. In terms of evaluating the utility and reliability of the vast range of data available on the World Wide Web it poses a serious challenge to the historian. It is easy to type a word into the 'search' box of an Internet search engine such as Google or Yahoo, press the return button and instantly be presented with thousands of hits relating to your particular query. It can be daunting trying to decide which site to visit, the brief description offering only a very limited glimpse of what information the site might contain. Much time can be lost in visits to unfruitful sites and in trying to pick out those sections of relevance in others.

Once you have been successful and found relevant information you must subject it to the same rigorous process of analysis and evaluation that you would do when researching information from books, journals and newspapers. Evaluating Internet sources can be difficult because anyone can place what he or she wants to on the Internet and there is no way of monitoring the accuracy of the information. The best you can do is to ask a series of basic questions such as the ones shown overleaf.

It is becoming increasingly common for students to visit online encyclopaedia sites such as Wikipedia. Created as recently as 2001 Wikipedia is a web-based free encyclopaedia, which has grown into one of the largest reference web sites available to students. However, its size does not mean that all the information it carries is accurate and reliable. When using the information from web sites such as Wikipedia it is important to bear some basic points in mind:

* Once an entry has been made it can be altered by anyone who visits that site;
* People can add to, change and even delete part of the original entry;
* The log at the end of the article will tell you when the last alteration was made;
* The problem with such a site is ensuring that all the information listed is factually accurate and not subject to distortion or deliberate bias;
* What is unknown is the calibre and status of the people who have contributed information to the article.

When assessing the reliability of a website a clue can be obtained from the actual web address. Some of the most common suffixes (endings) to web addresses are as follows:

> * **.edu**   a website hosted by an educational institution. You would expect such information to be scholarly and researched.
>
> * **.gov**   a website hosted by a government body. You would expect the information to be accurate but it could well contain biased information as the government body wishes to portray itself in a favourable light.
>
> * **.org**   a website hosted by an organisation or society. The accuracy of the information will depend upon the reputation of the organisation or society and how you feel about that body.
>
> * **.com**   a website hosted by a commercial organisation. You need to be careful and watch out for purpose and bias.

Objectivity
- What is the purpose of the website?
- Is its purpose commercial, political, religious etc?
- Look for clues in the suffix to the web address. E.g. Does it end in .edu, .gov, .org, .com?
- Do you trust the author or organisation providing the information?
- Is there advertising on the page?

Coverage
- Is the topic covered in depth?
- Are the links to the site comprehensive?
- How useful is the information for the topic under study?

Authority
- Does the information come from a reputable website?
  E.g. BBC education
- Who has ownership of the material?

Questions to ask when evaluating an Internet source

Currency
- When was the website last updated?
- Is the website still being maintained? This can influence accuracy, e.g. medical and travel information needs to be updated regularly for it to be accurate.

Accuracy of information
- How accurate is the material likely to be?
- Are there any obvious signs of bias attached to the site?
- Can you tell how well researched the information is?
- Does the author cite the sources of information used in the writing of this site?

Authorship
- Who is the author of the source?
- Was the information compiled by an individual or an organisation?
- If it was an organisation is there any obvious motive?
- Is the author an expert in that field?

What difficulties do Historians face when using sources as pieces of evidence?

The first question to be asked is: Can this source be trusted? If not, then your next step is to consider why. A favourite conclusion among candidates is to suggest that the source cannot be trusted because 'it is biased'. Candidates often write down that a source is biased but they seldom show any understanding of what they mean by bias or explain why they think the source is biased.

What is bias?

- Bias is one-sidedness.
- A source is biased if it favours one side or gives one particular view of an event.
- Bias can be found in most historical sources, to varying degrees and for different reasons.
- Historians need to be aware of bias and take it into account when using a source.
- A biased source can still be useful to an historian.

Reasons for bias in sources:

- Intentional bias – when a source is deliberately distorted or falsified, such as missing out important facts or treating views as facts;
- Limited access to material – when a piece is written before the full nature of the subject becomes clear, which could result in a one-sided account;
- Beliefs or feeling of the author – such feelings or beliefs can blind the author from giving a reasoned and objective view;
- Particular purpose behind a source – speeches are usually delivered for a political reason; newspaper articles often have a political agenda behind them; adverts are intended to persuade the viewer.

If a source is clearly one-sided, you should ask yourself 'What is the other side?'

Other problems areas include:

- Documents can be altered through words being taken out or put in.
  E.g. The sentence 'The rescue of the soldiers from the beaches of Dunkirk was a triumph of deliverance' has a completely different meaning if you add the word 'not' before the words 'triumph of deliverance'.
- Sources can be faked.
  E.g. In 1983 the academic world was shocked by the 'discovery' of the Hitler Diaries which were immediately serialised in *The Sunday Times*. When subjected to forensic examination they were found to be a modern fake, yet they had fooled many eminent historians who had wanted to believe that they were true.
- They can be quoted out of context or misquoted.
  E.g. MPs often claim that they have been quoted out of context, accusing the press of taking a section of their speech or interview and viewing it in isolation without any reference to what was said immediately before or after it. This can dramatically alter the meaning of what the MP was actually saying.

- They can be copied inaccurately.
  E.g. When the 1901 Census went on line in 2001 the Public Record Office was immediately emailed with complaints of inaccurate transcriptions form the original documents. Much of the work had be‹ performed in India by persons who were not familiar with British names or their spellings. Such errors could impact upon family historians researching genealogy.
- Illustrations can be completely imaginary.
  E.g. Artists can be commissioned to create a representation of a battle scene such as this image of th‹ battle of Rhuddlan Marsh, fought in 795 AD, between the Welsh and the Saxons.

- Photographs can be deliberately altered.

This original photograph shows Stalin (middle) walking next to Nikolai Yezhov (right), the chief of th‹ secret police. He was responsible for dealing with all opposition to Stalin.

This altered photograph was issued a few years after the original. In 1938 Yezhov was arrested durin‹ a purge ordered by Stalin. After Yezhov's fall from power the picture was adapted to remove him.

Detecting bias in historical sources and the reasons for it. Study the following sources and then answer the questions that follow.

Source A

Well I remember, how in early years,

I toil'd therein, with unavailing tears;

Condemn'd to suffer what I could not shun,

Till Sol seven times his annual course had run!

No bondage state – no inquisition cell,

Nor scenes yet dear to the Prince of Hell,

Could greater acts of cruelty display

Than yon tall factories on a former day;

E'en neighbouring forests frow'd with angry nods,

To see, Oppression! thy demand for rods!

Rods, doom'd to bruise in barb'rous dens of noise

The tender forms of orphan girls and boys!

Whose cries – which mercy in no instance found,

Were by the din of whirling engines drown'd.

But all is past! and may Treffynnon [Holywell] see

No more of fell Prestonian tyranny!

John Jones, 'Poems' (Manchester, 1856).

As a child in the early nineteenth century John Jones of Llanasa worked in the cotton mills of Christopher Smalley, which were situated in the Greenfield Valley below Holywell in Flintshire. Smalley's father had moved to Holywell from Lancashire hence the reference to Preston.

Source B

'All the cotton-mills on the river go under the name of the Cotton Twist Company. It is to Mr. Christopher Smalley, one of the partners, and eldest son to the founder of these great manufactories, I am obliged for the account of what relates to them.

The cotton-twist company have between three and four hundred apprentices, which they clothe and feed themselves, in commodious houses built for that purpose, the boys and girls in separate houses. These houses are white-washed twice every year, are fumigated three times a week through every apartment, with smoak of tobacco; besides this the sleeping-rooms are washed twice a week, and the bed-stocks are frequently sprinkled with rectified oil of tar. All the windows in the sleeping-rooms open at the tops, by which a thorough draft of air is admitted during the whole time the children are at work. To these and other precautions the good state of health of so many children may be justly attributed; for though the number of apprentices have not been less than 300 for these seven years past, they have only buried seven. Their food for dinner is beef or pork and potatoes, or soup and bread and cheese, as much as they please to eat. Their breakfasts and suppers in summer is milk and bread; in the winter, when milk cannot be had, they drink porridge or broth, with bread and cheese. A surgeon is appointed to superintend their health; and a Sunday school is regularly attended by a master at each house.'

Thomas Pennant, *The History of the Parishes of Whiteford and Holywell* (1796). As a landowner in the Holywell area Pennant rented out land in the Greenfield Valley to a number of industrialists and he was a good acquaintance of Christopher Smalley. Smalley provided Pennant with this information in a letter.

Source C

An engraving showing three large cotton mills which stretched down the Greenfield Valley below Holywell parish church. These mills employed many hundreds of workers – men, women and children. This engraving appeared in Pennant's *History of the Parishes of Whiteford and Holywell* (1796).

Questions:

(a) Study Sources A-C. Compare and contrast the descriptions of the living and working conditions of children employed in the cotton mills in the Greenfield Valley in the late eighteenth and early nineteenth centuries.

(b) In what ways do the sources exhibit elements of bias in their recording of living and working conditions in the cotton mills? Can you suggest reasons for such bias?

(c) Are such biased sources of any use to the historian studying the cotton industry in Greenfield Valley?

What types of evaluation will you be expected to perform at AS and A Level?

1. Comprehension of the content of a source

The comprehension question is designed to test your understanding of the content of the source. It is usually the first question and therefore carries the lowest mark allocation. To be successful at comprehension you need to ask yourself a number of questions relating to the source:

- What does the source actually tell us?
- What information can be gleaned from the attribution?

Look beyond the obvious and attempt to read between the lines – see what you can infer from the source.

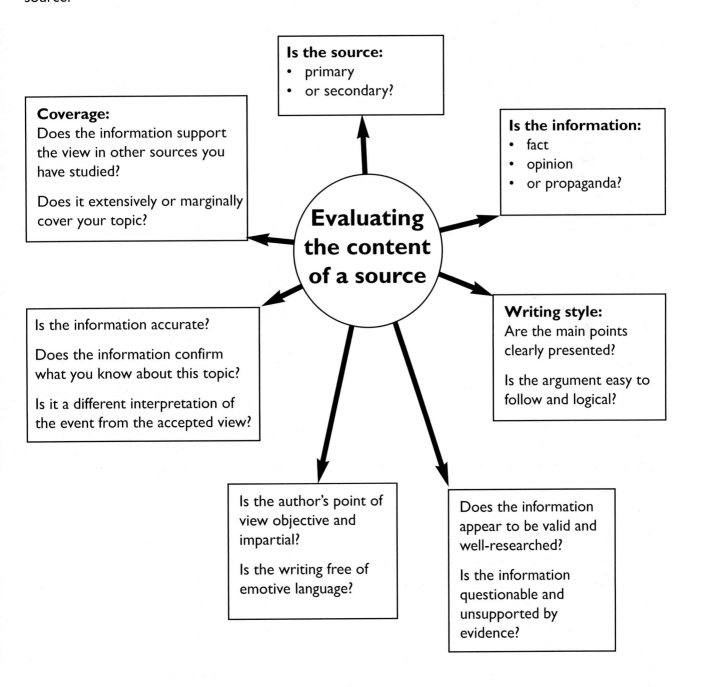

Is the source:
- primary
- or secondary?

Coverage:
Does the information support the view in other sources you have studied?

Does it extensively or marginally cover your topic?

Is the information:
- fact
- opinion
- or propaganda?

Evaluating the content of a source

Is the information accurate?

Does the information confirm what you know about this topic?

Is it a different interpretation of the event from the accepted view?

Writing style:
Are the main points clearly presented?

Is the argument easy to follow and logical?

Is the author's point of view objective and impartial?

Is the writing free of emotive language?

Does the information appear to be valid and well-researched?

Is the information questionable and unsupported by evidence?

2. Evaluating the attribution of a source

The origin of a source can have a major impact upon both its reliability and usefulness and needs to be subjected to the same close evaluation as the content. The diagram below provides a summary on how this can be achieved.

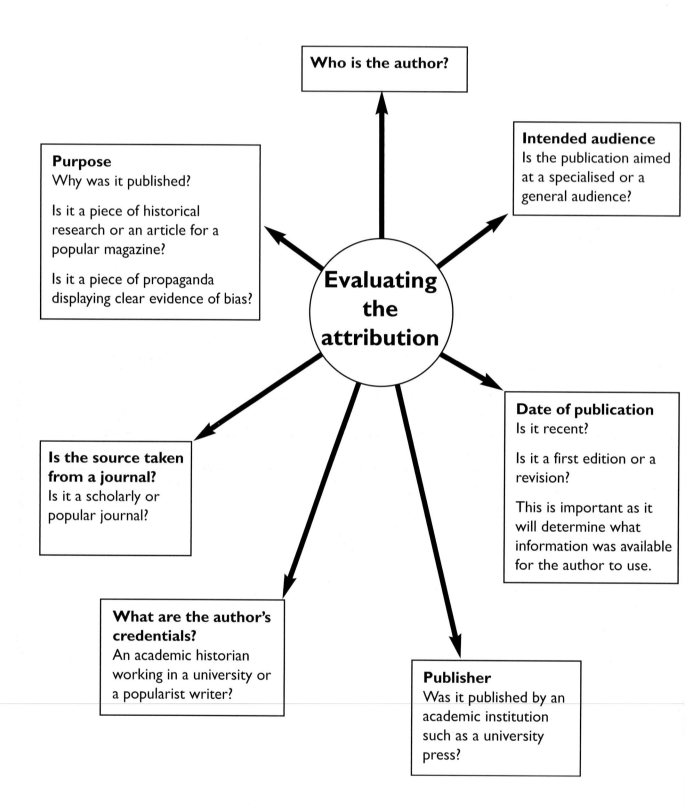

Who is the author?

Intended audience
Is the publication aimed at a specialised or a general audience?

Purpose
Why was it published?

Is it a piece of historical research or an article for a popular magazine?

Is it a piece of propaganda displaying clear evidence of bias?

Evaluating the attribution

Is the source taken from a journal?
Is it a scholarly or popular journal?

Date of publication
Is it recent?

Is it a first edition or a revision?

This is important as it will determine what information was available for the author to use.

What are the author's credentials?
An academic historian working in a university or a popularist writer?

Publisher
Was it published by an academic institution such as a university press?

3. Placing the source in its historical context

This is a key requirement at both AS and A Level and it demands that you examine the source in relation to the bigger picture. Placing a source in its historical context means linking it to the wider scene, examining its place and significance in the broader chronology of events. Basic questions need to be asked such as:

- Does the source provide a narrow focus or a broad view of events?

- Does it focus on a single issue and miss out certain other issues?

- Does it emphasise or exaggerate one issue at the expense of others?

- Does its coverage provide a distorted interpretation of the time period or event?

Analogy

The source can be considered to be one piece of a large jigsaw puzzle. You have been provided with that one piece and need to show how it relates to the rest of the jigsaw. You need to be able to relate that piece to the 'bigger picture', which requires detailed knowledge of the period. This is what is known as placing the source in its historical context. For example the scene on the jigsaw might show Hitler's consolidation of power 1933-34 which is mapped out in stages. You have been given the piece of the jigsaw that shows just one stage of this consolidation process such as the Enabling Law. You will need to use your knowledge of this topic to show it does not give the full picture but only one stage, and that it fails to show other important stages such as the Reichstag fire, the Night of the Long Knives and the creation of the office of Führer. If you have a good knowledge of this period you will be able to give the 'bigger picture' in order to complete the jigsaw. If you lack this background knowledge you can do little more than comment upon the source itself.

4. Considering the usefulness of a source

Questions at AS and A Level often ask candidates to consider the usefulness of a piece of evidence. When judging usefulness you should ask a series of probing questions about the source.

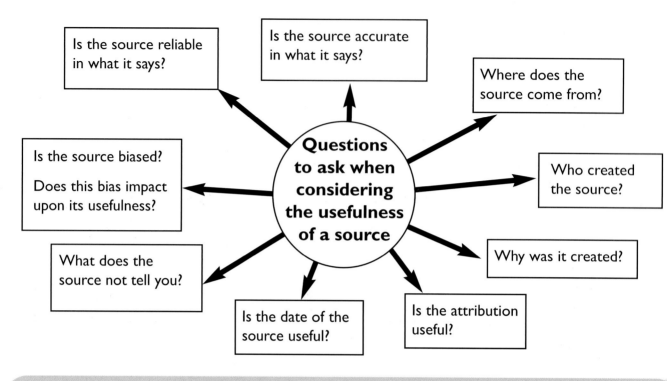

Is the source reliable in what it says?

Is the source accurate in what it says?

Where does the source come from?

Is the source biased? Does this bias impact upon its usefulness?

Questions to ask when considering the usefulness of a source

Who created the source?

Why was it created?

What does the source not tell you?

Is the date of the source useful?

Is the attribution useful?

Your task

'This agitation has arisen from a deep-rooted objection to an 'alien' church, and includes but a small minority of the inhabitants. The payment of tithes to this Church is also considered to be a badge of conquest, which we are determined to shake off with as little delay as possible. The present state of agriculture is not the cause but the occasion of this agitation – the farmers being obliged to look for reductions in both rent and tithe to save themselves from further ruin. They are fully justified in appealing to the clergy for reductions as well as to their landowners. Those clergy who have refused to grant the appeals of the farmers and have distrained [seized] their stock and refused to sell them by public auction, are mainly responsible for these disturbances… The Church authorities have grossly insulted and exasperated my fellow-countrymen by calling for the assistance of the Military and Police to protect them while securing the full payment of their tithes.'

Evidence given by Thomas Gee to a Committee of Enquiry into the Tithe Agitation in Wales in 1887. Gee was a Nonconformist preacher in a Welsh Calvinistic chapel in Denbigh and he was also the editor of a radical newspaper, which printed articles calling on local farmers to oppose the payment of the tithe.

Apply the questions listed in the diagram above to consider the usefulness of this source to an historian investigating the causes of the Tithe War in north-east Wales in the late 1880s.

5. Considering the reliability of a source.

At AS and A Level, you will be expected to assess the reliability of a source as a piece of evidence. When considering reliability you should consider the following:

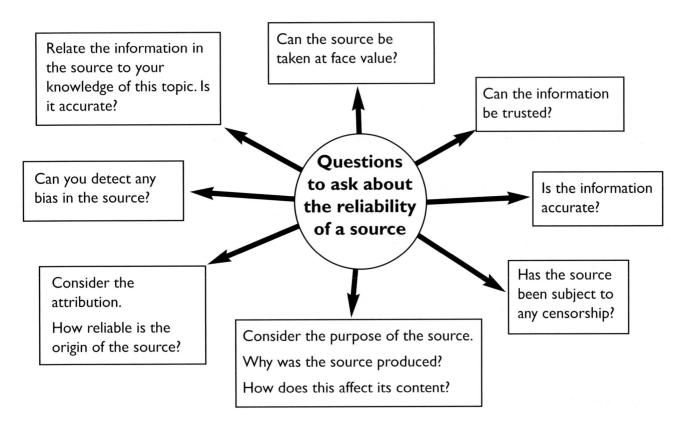

6. Source comparison or cross-referencing

Candidates will be expected to make comparison between sources, to identify similarities and differences. This is known as cross-referencing. It means making inferences from both sources and working out what the writers of the sources are suggesting. A favoured approach to the cross-referencing of sources is to:

- Read both sources carefully, underlining key words, terms or phrases;
- Make use of these key words in the answer;
- Avoid copying out large sections of the source; quote small sections of a sentence to illustrate or demonstrate the meaning of the author;
- Make sure the reader is aware of the source you are referring to by using such phrases as 'Source A suggests that ...' or 'the author of Source B believes that ...'
- Examine both attributions. Note the dates of the two sources, are they primary or secondary sources? Who wrote them?
- Does the standpoint of the author suggest any possible bias in the source?

Test your understanding of this chapter

Read each of the statements listed below and state whether you think they are true or false, giving full reasons for your decision.

Statement	True	False	Reasons for your choice
Eyewitness accounts are always more useful than those written by historians			
Biased sources are of no use to the historian			
Cartoons have no value because they are always one-sided			
Photographs are always a true representation of what happened			
The work of historians are more trustworthy because they are likely to have been researched			
A photograph is only useful if you know exactly when it was taken and by whom			
Letters to friends are likely to contain a person's real thoughts			
Diaries are the best sources of information for the biographer			
Information obtained from the internet cannot be relied upon to be accurate			
Historical novels are of no use to the historian			
Newspapers provide evidence of what people were thinking at that time			

Statement	True	False	Reasons for your choice
Government statistics cannot be relied upon			
History books can be trusted to give a balanced view of events			
All sources are biased in one form or another			
Speeches are usually biased since they are trying to persuade an audience			
Oral history is of little use to the historian			
Deathbed confessions are always true			
A source is only useful if it is reliable			
Illustrations that are imaginary are of no value to the historian			

CHAPTER FOUR

DEMONSTRATING THE SKILLS OF THE HISTORIAN
Interpretations and representations

Interpreting historical writing

Richard Cobb, a leading historian of the French Revolution, has written that the principal aim of the historian 'is to make the dead live'. To achieve this historians have to investigate the past and, using the evidence available to them, make reasoned judgements and assumptions about how and why events happened in the way they did. In doing so they interpret the past. It is a process of reflection, looking back on events with the benefit of hindsight.

How one historian interprets an event may be very different from how another historian interprets that same event. At AS and A Level you will be expected to understand the **process of how and why** the historian reached a particular interpretation. In doing so you will be addressing the key requirements of **Assessment Objective 2b**, which requires you to:

'... *analyse and evaluate, in relation to the historical context, how aspects of the past have been interpreted and represented in different ways.*'

Many of the topics you will study in your AS and A Level course will have generated considerable controversy and be subject to a wide variety of interpretations by historians. It will be your task to demonstrate an awareness and understanding of the main lines of debate among historians in the topic area you are studying, and you will be expected to evaluate the arguments for and against particular interpretations. In many respects you are acting like a judge, hearing the various arguments and giving a summation of them, before deciding upon your own viewpoint.

Judge and jury listen to:

Interpretation of events by the defence barrister

Interpretation of events by the prosecution barrister

Judge then gives a summation of both interpretations to the jury

In many respects the process you will go through when analysing and evaluating how and why a particular event has been interpreted differently is similar to what goes on in a Crown Court. A jury of twelve people sit at the side of the court and listen to the interpretation of events presented by two barristers, one acting for the defence, the other for the prosecution. They will present different and sometimes contrasting interpretations of how and why things happened in the manner they did. At the end of both presentations the judge will provide the jury with a summation in which the key points of each side of the case are outlined. The jury will then be sent away and asked to decide which interpretation of events they believe to be the most accurate.

At AS and A Level you will be expected to act like this Crown Court judge providing the examiner with a reasoned account of how and why particular interpretations were arrived at, and providing your own reasoned judgement about which interpretation you believe to be most accurate. In contrast to a court of law, however, historians are sometimes faced with more than two interpretations to weigh up.

Before proceeding further it would be useful to define what is meant by the terms interpretation and representation.

What is an interpretation?

The Oxford English Dictionary defines interpretation as '... the action of explaining the meaning of something.' It is the action of interpreting how and why events happened in the manner that they did.

E.g. Explaining why England and Wales erupted into Civil War in 1642.

What is a representation?

A representation has been defined as an attempt to give an impression of an aspect of history.

E.g. Reconstruction of a battle scene by the Sealed Knot society or a museum's selection of artefacts to represent a scene from the past.

In this respect both interpretations and representations are conscious attempts to explain the past. Such explanations are based upon a wide variety of source material such as paintings, photographs, films, poems, plays, oral accounts, physical remains such as buildings and sites, museums, the considered views of historians as well as the accounts of people who are remembering past events. In the last instance their recollection might not be as ordered or considered as that of an academic historian but it is still valid. The essential characteristic of any interpretation or representation is that it is a conscious attempt by the author, artist, producer etc to present a particular view of the past. This may be very different from those of others.

When considering how and why such interpretations or representations were formed you may be required to further your investigation with a consideration of historiography. This will require you to examine how historians have differed in their interpretations and the reasons for those differences. They may have been writing at different times or their interpretations might reflect a particular political, religious or economic standpoint they feel strongly about. Only after you have gone through this process of investigation can you reach a judgement as to the usefulness and reliability of an interpretation or representation as a piece of historical evidence.

Historiography

Historiography is important at both AS and A Level. It is the study of how the history of a particular event has been written, and how successive generations of historians have re-interpreted the past, sometimes in sharply contrasting ways.

E.g. Historians may have contrasting views about how the generals directed the war effort on the Western Front during the First World War, and those views will have changed over the decades or as a result of a different generation of historians studying the evidence.

AS and A Level assessments on interpretations and representations are likely to encourage you to concentrate on:

- The process by which the interpretation or representation was created;

- The source material available to the creator of the interpretation or representation;

- How this interpretation or representation was affected by the views or values of the historian or artist who composed it;

- The context of the work – the date when it was produced, by whom it was produced and the circumstances under which it was produced;

- The purpose of the work – why was it produced, was it commissioned or was it freelance?

- The intended audience – for whom was it produced, was it for a general audience or a specialist audience?

- The validity or otherwise of this work.

Various tasks will be used by the Awarding Bodies to test your understanding and application of the above methods and processes. These could include the analysis and evaluation of sources, both written and visual, in an attempt to get you to identify and explain the interpretations. It could involve the evaluation of a particular representation such as a novel, a film or a reconstruction, or it could demand that you consider different interpretations or representations of the same event or site, whether that is a consideration of contemporary or later reflections or both. It may be that such exercises are more suited to internal assessment investigations than to written assessments under timed examination conditions since this will allow for more in-depth analysis and evaluation.

Dealing with representations

Whatever the representation its creator, whether it be a writer, a filmmaker, an artist or a museum curator, would have gone through a process of research and investigation in order to gather evidence from which to generate that visual or written image. When evaluating the accuracy of that representation it is important that you ask yourself several important questions about how it was created.

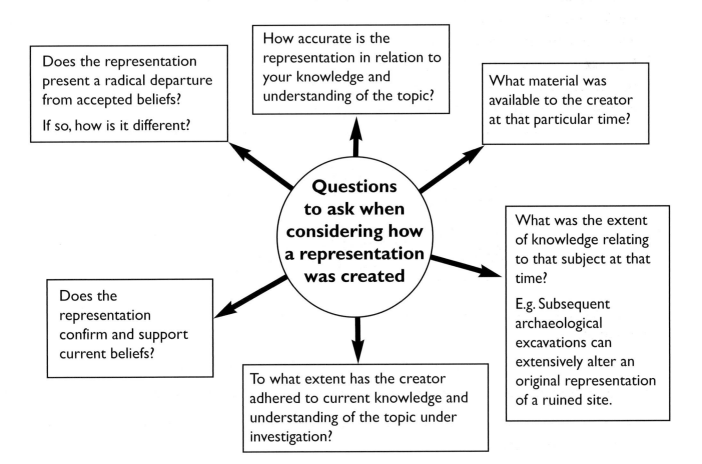

When considering the utility and reliability of a representation to an historian it is therefore very important that you investigate the process by which it was created, as the following example of the Roman amphitheatre at Caerleon illustrates.

Example of creating a visual representation from archaeological evidence:

The Roman amphitheatre at Caerleon

Photograph of Mortimer Wheeler's excavation of Caerleon amphitheatre in 1927.

Alan Sorrell's representation of the amphitheatre at Caerleon. This image was created in the early 1930s following Mortimer Wheeler's excavation.

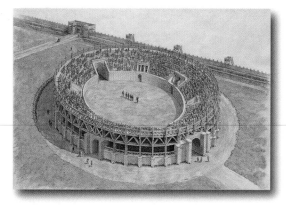

An artist's impression of the Caerleon amphitheatre as it may have appeared in the late first century AD. John Banbury drew this representation for the Cadw guidebook of the site, which was published in the late 1990s.

Between 1926-27 the archaeologist Mortimer Wheeler undertook extensive excavations at Caerleon to uncover its Roman amphitheatre; subsequent excavations by V. E. Nash-Williams of the National Museum of Wales followed. The museum was anxious to present its findings to the public and commissioned the graphic artist Alan Sorrell to execute a visual representation of what the amphitheatre would have looked like in Roman times, based upon its current archaeological remains. In order to complete his visual image Sorrell carried out extensive research work as well as receiving the expert knowledge and guidance of the archaeologists.

Since the time that Alan Sorrell created his image additional excavations of the site have been undertaken. The information obtained from these and comparative information gathered from similar sites in Roman towns across the country, have served to change the way archaeologists think the building was constructed. In recent years there have been major advances in scientific methods such as the use of geophysics, a type of radar which plots the layout of walls and debris lying unseen below the surface, and the use of Carbon 14 dating to give a more precise chronology. An excavation in 1962 indicated a timber superstructure for the amphitheatre and this later discovery was incorporated by John Banbury, a graphic artist commissioned by Cadw to prepare illustrations for its new guide book to the Roman remains at Caerleon. His representation therefore differs from that of Sorrell.

Films are sometimes used as an educational tool to help illustrate a particular period or event in time. Pupils in Year 9, for instance, are often shown the film *All Quiet on the Western Front* or *Hedd Wyn* to provide them with greater insight into the conditions faced by British soldiers fighting in the trenches in Flanders. Alongside this they could be shown the last episode of *Blackadder Goes Forth*, and they could be asked to test the accuracy of the representations they have been shown against their knowledge and understanding of the topic. They could be asked to consider why the representations differ and this will involve them examining the motives of the creator and the intended audience. They could also be asked to consider the process by which the creator investigated the events prior to making the film or programme.

At A Level this process would be undertaken in a much more sophisticated and detailed fashion. An alternative to using film would be a site visit to a museum to investigate whether a particular reconstruction or selection of a group of artefacts gives an accurate representation of the scene it claims to portray. For example, you could make a site visit to Big Pit in Blaenavon and undertake an investigation as to whether this gives an accurate representation of the working conditions of Welsh miners during the early twentieth century.

Why do historians come up with different interpretations?

When investigating the past historians may well have access to different materials and this can have a decisive influence upon the judgements and conclusions they form. They may be writing from a particular standpoint, be it political, economic, religious, cultural or social. In this context their evaluation of sources and their selection of the most useful ones will be influenced by their own standpoints. They may be targeting particular audiences and so would slant their interpretation accordingly, or they may be writing during different periods of history and therefore be reflecting the particular views of that period.

Example: How have historians viewed the causes of the French Revolution of 1789?

The storming of the Bastille

The basic fact that France experienced a revolution in 1789 that resulted in the collapse of its monarchy and a fundamental change in the political direction of the country, which resulted in the establishment of a republic, cannot be disputed. What can be disputed, however, are the causes of this dramatic event and why events unfolded in the manner that they did. Ever since 1789 historians have interpreted the causes of the revolution in different ways, often according to whether they approve or disapprove of the revolution.

Marxist interpretation

Marxist historians see the Revolution as a series of class-based struggles that resulted in the rise to prominence of what Karl Marx termed the proletariat or working class. Such a view dominated all thought on the causes of the Revolution throughout the first half of the twentieth century, the leading historian of this interpretation being Georges Lefebvre who viewed the Revolution as a bourgeois revolution. As a result of the Industrial Revolution and associated economic development the bourgeoisie or middle class had become a powerful body that found themselves denied access into the political sphere by the powerful and privileged class of the French nobility. The Revolution was seen as an attempt by the bourgeoisie to obtain equal rights and was therefore viewed as a class struggle. Other left-wing historians who supported this 'social interpretation' were Albert Soboul and George Rude.

Revisionist interpretation

Revisionist historians writing since the 1950s have rejected the socialist interpretation of a class struggle. Instead they have tended to concentrate upon the importance of political factors as the chief cause of the Revolution. They have argued that events such as the American War of Independence helped to influence the French philosophes to demand more democratic change within France. This was the age of the Enlightenment and philosophes such as Rousseau helped to undermine the security of the Ancien Regime (the established system of government) by calling for reform. Alfred Cobban, a Professor of History in the University of London, first put such a revisionist interpretation forward in the 1950s and early 1960s and later historians such as Francois Furet developed his ideas further in the 1970s.

Most recent interpretations

Over the last two decades some historians have begun to step back from the Revisionist interpretation and have identified weaknesses in both the interpretations outlined above. In the 1990s the historian Gwynne Lewis attempted a synthesis of the two interpretations. In his book *The French Revolution: Rethinking the Debate* he refers to weaknesses in the arguments of both the Marxist stress upon social and economic factors, and upon the Revisionist stress upon cultural and political factors as being the chief causes of the Revolution. According to Lewis and his supporters the causes were many and varied and really involved a combination of the factors drawn from the two main interpretations.

Your task

What are the main historical interpretations or schools of thought for the period you are currently studying at AS or A2?

It is therefore important that you are able to identify the standpoint of the author of the source you are studying in order to be able to critically evaluate their interpretation and place it into context. The information that will enable you to perform this task will be in the attribution, the reference below the source that identifies the author, names the publication from which the source is extracted and gives the date of its publication.

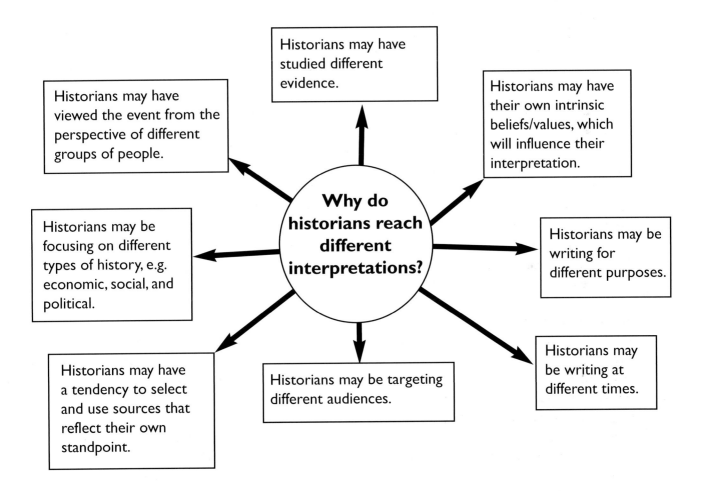

Your task

Can you identify other factors which can influence the interpretation adopted by an historian?

Factors that can influence the interpretation formulated by an historian

1. The availability of material

A good historian will attempt to uncover all the evidence available but this will depend upon the place and time in which they are writing. Many factors can influence the availability of material and this in turn can have a major impact upon the interpretation that is presented, as the following examples demonstrate:

(i)   Changing political situations can affect the access to manuscripts. Until the 1990s, for instance, western historians writing about the Second World War would only have had access to manuscript material deposited in the archives of the countries of western Europe and the USA, and so their interpretations were sometimes limited because they lacked access to the vast archives of manuscripts confiscated by the Russians at the end of the war. The fall of communism in Eastern Europe in the early 1990s suddenly opened up a new arena of research opportunities, and this has led to a reappraisal of aspects of the Second World War as well as aspects of Soviet history.

For example, until the early 1990s western historians had assumed that Hitler had committed suicide in his bunker but could never prove it. The opening up of the Soviet archives resulted in the finding of a file on Hitler's death that had been prepared for Stalin, which contained concrete evidence of Hitler's suicide in April 1945. It also contained his dental records, a section of his jaw with unique bridgework to his teeth and the top part of his skull with an exit wound for a single bullet shot, thus helping to confirm the historian Hugh Trevor-Roper's original theory, dating back to 1947, that Hitler had shot himself through his right temple. In this instance the new evidence helped to confirm an existing interpretation of events.

(ii)   In Britain there is a thirty-year rule, which governs the release into the public domain of all official government papers. This came into force in the 1960s and replaced a former fifty-year classification of official documentation. As a result of such restrictions historians working on a history of the Falklands War of 1982, for example, will be limited in their access to official papers, and while they will have access to accounts printed in the newspapers these will have been subjected to censorship. They will not be able to consult cabinet papers until their release in 2012 but even then some sensitive documents could still be withheld from public view. Historians writing after 2012 will have far greater access to official papers than those writing before and consequently their interpretation may be very different from the writings of historians before this date.

(iii)   Families may hold back 'private papers' of individuals until after their deaths, and in some instances for several generations. Thus the historian compiling a biography of a notable politician would not be able to complete a comprehensive study unless they had access to private papers, such as diaries and family letters, in which personal details are revealed.

What evidence is available and the extent to which that evidence is examined will have a dramatic influence upon the interpretation that is reached. As the historian E. H. Carr noted:

> 'The facts are really not at all like fish on the fishmonger's slab. They are like fish swimming about in a vast and sometimes inaccessible ocean; and what the historian catches will depend, partly on chance, but mainly on what part of the ocean he chooses to fish in and what tackle he chooses to use.'
>
> E. H. Carr, *What is History?* [1961]

Your task

(a) Explain the meaning of the quotation from the work of the historian E. H. Carr.

(b) What does this quotation suggest about the accuracy of the views of historians?

2. Writing at different times

Historians are naturally influenced or conditioned by the times in which they live. The work of the historian often mirrors the society in which he or she works. That is why it is very important to consider the date of publication of the source. The attribution will often provide a vital clue in helping you reach a verdict about the interpretation that is presented in the source.

For example, Whig historians of the late nineteenth century were writing at a time when the British Empire was at its height, encompassing a third of the world's population. They wrote history that reflected this impression that Britain, and the liberal British political institutions, had evolved to be the best and were therefore examples to be copied by the rest of the world. Their views were very different from historians writing in the 1950s and 1960s when the Empire had been dismantled, and by the political climate of the twenty-first century such viewpoints seem to be very old-fashioned and dated.

In a similar way American historians writing in the 1950s during the McCarthy era were heavily influenced in their views of the Soviet Union by the anti-communist phobia that gripped America during that decade. They therefore tended to portray the Soviet Union in a very negative almost sinister light.

3. Historians can and do hold different ideological standpoints

When writing about the past historians can be influenced by their own political backgrounds and beliefs. Some historians, for example, are influenced by Marxist theories of history and will attempt to explain historical developments by looking at changing economic relationships between different groups in societies. Karl Marx referred to this as the class struggle. Such an interpretation plays down the role of the individual in favour of the wider issue of the class struggle and identifies economic factors as the main driving force of change.

Historians with a nationalist interest will tend to write history from the standpoint of one country's point of view, emphasising the role of that country's contribution to developments. French, German and British historians, for example, may each slant their interpretation of the battle of Waterloo in 1815 to emphasise the importance of the contribution of their own country. Likewise when studying events in Wales between the two world wars it is possible to detect a noticeable bias in the writings of some Welsh nationalist historians who vent their frustration at the apparent lack of attention from the English Government to Wales' problems during the Depression. The 1920s witnessed the birth of Plaid Cymru as a political party and its members were angry with and critical of the actions of the Government, accusing them of ignoring the severe economic hardship evident across Wales; a view not shared by Government ministers at the time or by some later historians.

Other historians might tend to stress the role and significance of individuals in shaping history, interpreting their actions as playing a decisive role in the shaping and implementation of policy and in the outcome of events. Italian nationalist historians, for example, created the myth of Italian unification being based on the collaborative actions of the main players, Cavour, Garibaldi and Victor Emanuel. They played down the role of characters like Mazzini who was critical to the movement of the Risorgimento and paid little attention to the aid that was received from abroad, especially that from Napoleon III. Italian politicians engaged in the process of nation building encouraged this view.

Other historians may reject existing long-held interpretations and offer a completely new view of an event or period, adopting what is termed a revisionist or radical interpretation. In the case of Italian unification the collapse of the Fascist state in 1945 led to a complete revision of the process of how Italy had come into being and was led by such historians as Denis Mack-Smith and L. C. B. Seaman. After the war they gained access to long-hidden documentation and used it to argue that Italy was united not because of collaboration but due to the conflict between the main players, each of which had their own agenda. Such an interpretation was a radical departure from the previous accepted interpretation and has now become the accepted version of how Italy was unified.

For discussion:

(a) Why might an historian writing in 1789 have a different view of the slave trade from an historian writing in 1989?

(b) Is the work of an historian known to hold strongly Marxist or nationalist views of any use to the student of A Level history?

Example: How has the Holocaust been interpreted by historians?

The origins of the Holocaust has been a matter of considerable debate among historians, especially since the trial of Adolf Eichmann in 1960 brought to the world's attention the true horrors of what had gone on inside the concentration camps operated by the Nazis during the Second World War. The different schools of thought can be summarised into the following groupings:

Auschwitz concentration camp

Intentionalist interpretation

Historians of the intentionalist school of thought have interpreted the Holocaust as part of a planned sequence of events, a deliberate policy that aimed to rid Europe of its Jewish population by mass extermination. According to the intentionalist view Hitler followed a 'master plan', a blue print for a systematic programme of persecution. His ideology and rhetoric throughout the 1920s and early 1930s demonstrated that it was always his intention to follow such a programme, and once in power his all-powerful totalitarian dictatorship ensured that his orders were carried out. From this standpoint it therefore follows that the initiation for the Holocaust came from above with the orders being issued by Hitler himself. Leading historians of this interpretation include Lucy Dawidowicz and Andreas Hillgruber.

Functionalist or Structuralist interpretation

Functionalist or structuralist historians dismiss the idea that there was a plan for the Holocaust and believe that it developed as part of an evolutionary programme driven by the needs of war. They portray the Third Reich as being badly led, a regime littered with internal rivalries and a chaotic process of decision making, which constantly led to improvisation and radicalisation. These historians thus interpret the Holocaust as an evolutionary process of intensified persecution, which developed as the German war machine advanced ever deeper into Poland and then Russia. The Holocaust, in their view, was the reaction to a particular set of circumstances rather than a planned activity. They argue that the initiation came from below rather than from above and that it was driven from within the lower ranks of the German bureaucracy. Leading historians of the functionalist interpretation include Hans Mommsen and Martin Broszat.

Synthesis interpretation

Recent research has resulted in a synthesis interpretation, a merging of both the functionalist and intentionalist viewpoints. They have put forward the view that the Holocaust was the result of forces issuing from both above and below. They believe that Hitler lacked a master plan but was the decisive force behind the Holocaust. They see it as the end result of a process of 'cumulative radicalisation', the outcome of increasingly extreme rhetoric and competition among different Nazi agencies, which resulted in increasingly extreme policies. Leading historians of the synthesis interpretation include Yehuda Bauer and Ian Kershaw.

Holocaust denial

Opposed to all these interpretations is the extreme viewpoint of the Holocaust deniers who have used the historical evidence, or lack of it, to argue that the genocide of Europe's Jews did not take place, and that the Holocaust forms part of a myth created by western historians who have distorted the historical evidence. David Irving has promoted himself as one of the leading exponents of this radical viewpoint.

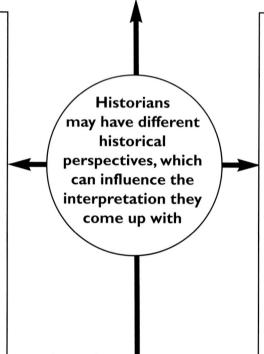

Importance of the individual
- Emphasis is placed upon the decisive role of the individual in history;
- A belief that history is made by 'great men and great women';
- Through their character they have shaped history while the masses play little or no role.

Revisionist interpretation
- This is an attempt to change commonly held ideas about the past and to challenge the accepted view of a particular period or event;
- It is the re-examination of historical facts with a view towards updating historical narratives with newly discovered, more accurate or less biased information;
- It presupposes that the history of an event, as it has traditionally been told, may not be entirely accurate;
- The assumption is that the interpretation of an historical event or period as it is accepted needs significant change.

Historians may have different historical perspectives, which can influence the interpretation they come up with

Marxist interpretation
- This is influenced by the views of Karl Marx;
- Marx emphasised the importance of explaining historical developments by looking at the changing economic relationships between different groups in society;
- The focus is on the economic relationship between classes rather than the importance of individuals;
- They tend to view history as determined, a movement towards an end state of a classless society.

Nationalist interpretation
- History written from a nationalist point of view will regard one nation as more important than others;
- Everything will emphasise the role of the nation;
- It often stresses the part played by individuals who are portrayed as heroes.

Your task

(a) What bullet points would you include in a box bearing the heading 'The Synthesis interpretation'?

(b) Can you identify other perspectives or attitudes which can influence the interpretations given by an historian?

Why do interpretations of historical events change over time?

1. Our understanding of history is constantly changing

If there were a universally accepted view of history that never changed there would be no need to research it further. The study of history is a continual process of interaction between the historian and the facts. Each generation of historians will tend to adopt its own interpretation and standpoint.

'History is a continual dialogue between the present and the past. Interpretations of the past are subject to change in response to new evidence, new questions asked of the evidence, new perspectives gained by the passage of time.'

[James McPherson, Pulitzer Prize winning historian]

2. Developments in other academic areas can cause the current accepted outlines of history to change

Advances in scientific investigation, most noticeably in DNA analysis, carbon dating, the analysis of tree rings and the examination of ice cores, have all had an impact on the interpretations adopted by historians. This new evidence may help to confirm established theories or it can present new evidence that undermines or rejects current established historical explanation.

Example: Modern scientific methods have helped to solve the mystery of what actually happened to Tsar Nicholas II of Russia, and his immediate family in July 1918

The Tsar and his family

Since 1918 historians have theorised about what actually happened to the Tsar and his family in July of that year when they suddenly disappeared. As the bodies of the Romanov family were never uncovered the events surrounding their fate had always remained a theory rather than solid fact. The accepted view was that they were all shot by Bolshevik soldiers on 17 July 1918 whilst under house arrest in the town of Ekaterinburg in the Urals. Yet several factors served to cast doubt on this theory, not least being the appearance of a lady claiming to be Anastasia, one of the Tsar's daughters. Another individual, a nurse named Natalya Mutnykh, claimed to have treated the Tsarina and four of her daughters four months after they were said to have been shot. Such events have served to question the accuracy of the interpretation that they had all been murdered in July 1918.

In 1991 the mutilated remains of several individuals thought to have been members of the Romanov family were discovered in a shallow grave along a road twelve miles north of Ekaterinburg. Dental records together with DNA tests carried out in Britain and the USA confirmed that the bodies were those of the Tsar, the Tsarina and three of their daughters, one of whom was Anastasia. The bodies of Alexei, the heir, and one of his sisters were missing. In 2007 the discovery of bones found in a burned area of ground near Ekaterinburg were subjected to a series of DNA tests. In April 2008 the bones were confirmed to be those of Alexei and his sister. The development of new scientific methods has thus served to close the ninety-year-old mystery of the missing Romanov family.

3. Changes in ideology over time

Changes and developments in political, economic, social and cultural fashions can have a dramatic effect upon how an historian interprets the past. Each generation has its own troubles and problems, and therefore its own interests and points of view. These often come to the forefront and influence how historians interpret the past.

Example: The historiography of the causes of the English Civil War

A re-enactment of a Civil War battle
© *English Heritage Photo Library*

Whig historians writing about the causes of the Civil War during Victorian times applied Charles Darwin's theory of evolution of man to the evolution of government from the authoritarian dominance of the medieval period through to the semi-constitutional government of Victorian times. They viewed the Civil War as an inevitable conflict between the interests of crown and parliament during the Seventeenth Century based upon religion and the rise to prominence of Puritanism and the redistribution of power that this entailed.

Marxist historians writing in the 1940s also viewed the Civil War as the inevitable result of the build up of many incidents but, unlike the Whig historians, they claim that social and economic factors were more to blame than religion. According to the Marxist historians it was the transition from a feudal economy to a bourgeois [gentry] state that caused the problems between crown and parliament, making the Civil War a 'class war'. The driving force of change came from social and economic issues, which then affected political and religious changes.

During the 1960s and 1970s these interpretations came under attack by a new school of **Revisionist historians** and today both Whig and Marxist interpretations have been overturned. Revisionist historians reject the belief in long-term causes and therefore inevitability. They see the main cause of the Civil War as the breakdown of trust between crown and parliament during the 1640s and place greater emphasis upon actual events during the late 1630s and early 1640s. For Revisionists the origins of the Civil War lie in the fact that Charles I made revolutionary changes to government that the conservative minded gentry could not accept. The result of these changes left the nation divided and hence the subsequent outbreak of civil war.

4. The accession of new data

The sudden availability of new types of information can have a dramatic impact upon the interpretation of events. It can confirm and, occasionally, overturn long held and established theories.

Example: A re-evaluation of the magnitude of the English victory in the Battle of Agincourt in 1415

Recent research by Professor Anne Curry has challenged the traditional view that English forces in the Battle of Agincourt were heavily outnumbered four to one by the French army and yet managed to pull off a stunning victory. Professor Curry has gone back to primary sources and examined the original enrolment records, documents that had not received much attention from previous historians. Using these documents she has been able to question the traditional interpretation of the battle. Her research has demonstrated that the difference in size between the two opposing forces was not as great, the French force comprising of 12,000 men compared to the English and

The battle of Agincourt

Welsh force of 8,000. This narrower gap obviously puts a different slant on the victory and Professor Curry has suggested that the numbers were originally exaggerated by English historians for patriotic reasons and had never really been questioned. Nobody had bothered to go back to the original documents to check that the figures were accurate.

5. The impact of revisionist theories

As time passes and influences change so do most historians' views on the explanation of historical events. Some historians, when attempting to explain how and why certain events in the past have occurred, might reject the traditional interpretation in favour of their own revised viewpoint.

'This is not why the war started.'

Example: A re-evaluation of military leadership during the First World War

The military leadership of British forces fighting in the trenches in Flanders during the First World War has frequently been condemned as poor by historians, common charges being that the generals commanding the army were blind to the realities of trench warfare, were ignorant of the conditions of their men and were unable to learn from their mistakes. Such a viewpoint led to the belief that the brave Tommies were the 'lions led by donkeys', a phrase often used to describe General Haig's leadership during the Battle of the Somme in 1916.

Soldiers engaging in battle in the trenches

During the 1960s revisionist historians like John Terraine began to challenge this interpretation. Historians are now less inclined to view the war in such a simplistic manner with brave soldiers being led to their slaughter by foolish officers. Historians such as Richard Holmes point out that the military leadership of the British army on the Western Front had to deal with many problems that they could not control, such as a lack of adequate military communications. Furthermore, military leadership improved throughout the war culminating in the Hundred Days offensive advance to victory in 1918. Thus many historians today conclude that the generals were doing as good a job as was possible under the extreme conditions that trench warfare entailed.

Your task

(a) Why is it important for historians to re-visit the interpretation of issues that have generated considerable historical debate?

(b) 'The re-evaluation of historical issues is a constant and necessary process.' How far do you agree or disagree with this view?

How can examiners assess your understanding of historical interpretations and representations?

1. Comparing different interpretations or representations of the same event

This type of question is common at A Level and involves you making a direct comparison between two sources, demonstrating your source evaluation skills and historical knowledge in order to reach a judgement about a particular interpretation. One source might be a contemporary viewpoint, the other an interpretation written after the event with the benefit of hindsight and research. The key focus will be to consider whether the contemporary source confirms or contradicts the interpretation given. Reference will also need to be made to the attribution or provenance of both sources, paying particular attention to the date when they were produced, the author, the type of publication and the possible purpose of the source. This will enable you to discuss how certain interpretations are arrived at. You will also be expected to consider the intended audience and why the account was written in the tone it was. You should conclude your answer with a direct reference back to the thrust of the question itself.

In the case of a comparative exercise of two representations, you should follow the same process of investigation and evaluation as the previously cited example of the drawings of Caerleon amphitheatre by two different artists illustrated.

Example: Comparison of a contemporary view with an interpretation

This question is focused upon the political changes in Wales following the Act of Union, 1536.

Source A

'The discord of old between England and Wales caused slaughters, invasions, enmities, burnings, poverty and such like fruits of war. But this Union engendered friendship, amity, love, alliance, assistance, wealth and quietness. God preserve and increase it.'

[From Rhys Meurig Y Cotrel, historian and gentleman landowner, writing in *Morganiae Archaiographia* (1578), by permission of the National Library of Wales.]

Source B

'...the supposition that it [Tudor policy] converted a land of wild anarchy into a perfect Paradise where ever since there has not been the slightest cause for complaint or the least deflection from that policy, is a matter for laughter.'

[From T. Gwynn Jones, a cultural historian, writing in an article called 'Cultural bases: a study of the Tudor period in Wales' in the Welsh magazine, *Y Cymmrodor* (1921), by permission of the National Library of Wales.]

Question:
Study Sources A and B. How far does Source A support or contradict the interpretation of the Act of Union given in Source B?

What is the Examiner looking for when marking this style of question?

The aim of the question is to assess the relationship between the contemporary view and the historian's interpretation. Both are sources but the historian (Source B) would have had access to Source A. In order to reach the top level of response in the mark scheme you would be expected to analyse and evaluate the content and provenance of each source in order to reach a substantiated judgement on the degree to which the source supports or contradicts a particular interpretation.

A developed response would identify that Source B is highly critical of the Union of Wales with England, and that it comments that the belief that the Union would solve the problem of lawlessness overnight was incorrect. Source A, in contrast, directly contradicts this interpretation by saying that the Union had a very positive effect in establishing a new era of friendship, prosperity and quietness. In terms of the provenance it would be noted that Source A was a contemporary view by a member of the Welsh gentry, a man who had much to gain from such a union. Source B, on the other hand, is the view of a modern historian who was writing with the benefit of hindsight. The best responses will conclude that historians like T. Gwynn Jones who are highly critical of the Acts of Union, would not find the evidence of Rhys Meurig Y Cotrel particularly useful in reaching their conclusions over Tudor policy in Wales.

A typical marking scheme applied by Examiners for assessing AO2b skills.

AO2b	Generic Level Descriptors
Level 1 ↓	• Answer demonstrates a limited understanding • Some discussion about the content of the sources; tends to be descriptive
Level 2 ↓	• Answer demonstrates a good understanding • Good discussion of the content of both sources, identifying the two interpretations • Some attempt to consider the attribution of both sources
Level 3	• Answer demonstrates a reasoned understanding • Sustained discussion of the content and provenance of each source • Will reach a substantiated judgement on the degree to which the sources support or contradict a particular interpretation

Your task

This question is focused upon the Civil War, 1642-1649.

Source A

'Upon the King's return to Oxford in 1642, there appeared nothing but dejection of mind, discontent, and secret mutiny; in the army, anger and jealousy amongst the officers, everyone accusing another of want of courage and conduct in the actions of the field; and they who were not of the army, blaming them all for their several failings and gross oversights.'

[From the pro-royalist Edward Hyde, Earl of Clarendon, writing in his book, *History of the Rebellion* (1667)]

Source B

'The Cavaliers marched in with such terror to the garrison and such gallantry that they startled not when one of their leading files fell before them all at once, but marched boldly over the dead bodies of their friends, under their enemies' cannon, and carried such valiant dreadfulness about them as made very courageous stout men recoil.'

[From an anonymous contemporary eyewitness account of a Royalist attack on Nottingham (1664)]

> **Question:**
> Study Sources A and B. How far does Source B support or contradict the interpretation given of the royalist army in Source A?
>
> *[Use the generic level descriptors listed in the chart opposite as a guide to help you compile your answer to this question.]*

2. An investigation into the validity of a representation

This type of question involves an investigation into the accuracy and therefore the validity of a particular representation. Such questions will invite you to:

- Outline the representation given and put it into its historical context;
- Examine how the creator was able to come up with that representation;
- Test the accuracy of the representation against other representations and your own knowledge and understanding of the period;
- Reach an overall judgement about the validity of the representation.

Such investigations are open to a range of questions, the following providing examples of some of the many variants:

Films: How far is the opening scene of the film *Saving Private Ryan* an accurate representation of the initial stages of the D Day landings in June 1944?

Steven Spielberg's film *Saving Private Ryan* was produced in 1998 and quickly secured international acclaim for its portrayal of a detachment of American soldiers on a special mission to search out and save a US soldier, Private James Ryan. The first thirty minutes of the film recreates the landing of US troops on the Normandy beaches on 6th June 1944, D Day. It is filmed through the eyes of an American soldier and as such provides graphic images of the landing and of the brutal realities of the attempts to secure a position on the beach against the onslaught of the German defences. The aim of the exercise is to test the accuracy and validity of this opening section of the film.

An image from the film showing American troops advancing up the beach to secure their landing.

Physical remains: How far is the restoration of the mansion house Plas Mawr in Conwy a true representation of the home of an Elizabethan gentleman?

During the 1990s Plas Mawr came under the care and management of Cadw and they undertook an extensive conservation programme of both the external and internal features of the house. Their aim was to recreate the house, as it would have looked when it was built for Robert Wynn during the 1580s.

In doing so they took care to ensure that original building techniques were used whenever possible, that the paint and decoration was representative of the Elizabethan age, as was all the furniture and household items placed in the various rooms. Cadw now claim that this is a true representation of the home of an Elizabethan gentleman living in the 1580s.

Photograph of the Great Chamber c. late 1580s, following the Cadw conservation of Plas Mawr.

TV documentaries: How far is the BBC documentary *Coal House* an accurate reflection of life in the South Wales mining communities in the late 1920s?

In October 2007 three families abandoned life in the twenty-first century to be transported back to life in the South Wales coalfield during 1927. It formed part of a BBC living history series, which followed the lives of the families over four weeks. It was centred on 1927, the year after the General Strike and before the nationalisation of the pits. The families lived in period-decorated cottages in Blaenavon that lacked all modern amenities. The men and boys over fourteen had to partake in a walk over the mountain to work the coal at Blaentillery No.2 mine, the last working coal mine of its kind in the UK. The women had to run the house under 1927 conditions, keeping the children and their husbands fed, watered and clean, using only food and household goods available at that time. The question asks you to evaluate whether this series of programmes generates an accurate reflection of life in the South Wales coal mining communities of the late 1920s.

Members of the three families living the *Coal House* experience, dressed in period costumes.

3. An investigation into how and why aspects of the past have been interpreted and represented in different ways

In the examination this type of question will take the form of an essay. You will be given a quote by an historian and you will be asked to say how far you agree with this interpretation and why. You will need to consider the processes that led to this particular interpretation and demonstrate an appreciation that some sort of selection of material has been made, and judge whether or not that selection is justified. For example, the essay may identify German military ambitions as being the main reason for the outbreak of war in 1914 and, using your historical knowledge of this period, you would be expected to weigh up this factor against other factors such as the growth of nationalism in the Balkans or the development of military alliances, which divided Europe into two armed camps, and reach a conclusion as to whether this interpretation of the causes of the First World War is a valid viewpoint.

More usually, however, this type of question forms part of an internal assessment exercise, which allows you to investigate an historical issue in much greater depth. This affords you the opportunity to explore differing interpretations and reach a sustained judgement as to the validity of those interpretations.

In internal assessment exercises you will be expected to:

- Demonstrate the skills of the historian as outlined in Chapters 2, 3 and 4 of this book;
- Comprehend, analyse and evaluate the ways in which the past has been interpreted or represented and show an understanding of the historical debate between historians;
- Undertake an investigation into an historical problem or issue about which there are a variety of viewpoints;
- Examine sources taken from the work of historians in order to assess and evaluate the interpretation that is presented;
- Demonstrate your ability to undertake personal research into a given topic;
- Analyse the sources critically and reach a conclusion about the validity of that particular interpretation or representation in the context of your historical knowledge of that period;
- Finally, after studying a range of sources and identifying the differing interpretations, you will be expected to demonstrate the ability to discriminate and reach a supported judgement as to which interpretation or representation is, in your view, most securely supported by the evidence.

The internal assessment task can be focused upon:

- An examination of how the reputation of an individual has changed over time;
- An examination of how the interpretation/representation of an historical event has changed over time;
- How historians, writing at the same time, have interpreted the same event in very different ways, and the reasons for this divergence of views.

Examples of historical issues that can generate debate and controversy over their interpretation/representation:

1. The extent to which the Catholic threat to Queen Elizabeth I between 1571 and 1588, both at home and abroad, has been exaggerated and in fact was dealt with relatively easily.
2. The extent to which King Louis XIV succeeded in establishing an absolute monarchy in France between 1661 and 1715.
3. The reasons why women in Britain were successful in obtaining political rights between 1867 and 1918.

4. The debate surrounding the causes of the Second World War – was its outbreak the result of a planned campaign of expansion by totalitarian regimes or was it an accident?

5. The extent to which the Holocaust formed part of a premeditated master plan to exterminate the Jewish population of Europe, as opposed to it being the result of cumulative radicalisation and the circumstances of war.

6. The extent to which there was a revolution in social, economic and foreign policy during the era of Margaret Thatcher, 1979-1990.

In each of these cases there will be a substantial element of debate amongst historians, some of whom will identify one factor as being more important than others, or who will see the process as part of a plan and therefore an intended outcome, as opposed to an unplanned, often accidental, sequence of events.

Example: Internal assessment exercise on the era of Margaret Thatcher in British politics

When investigating Margaret Thatcher's time as Prime Minister you would be expected to evaluate the evidence concerning the central issues of:

- The extent to which historians have attributed her rise to power as being due to the failings of the Labour government in the 1970s as opposed to the promises of changes espoused by the Conservatives;

- The extent to which the policies introduced by the Thatcher governments to deal with the economy, the welfare state and the trade unions amounted to a 'revolution' in government, or have such changes merely been over-exaggerated by some historians;

- The extent to which British foreign policy changed under Thatcher and whether this change amounted to a 'revolution' in style and policy direction;

- The debate about why Margaret Thatcher fell from power in 1990.

When considering such important questions historians will naturally present different interpretations and your task will be to identify and investigate these differing viewpoints and the reasons for them; to evaluate the strengths and weaknesses of the sources you have studied; to explain how and why these viewpoints may have changed over time, and to reach a substantiated judgement as to which interpretation is, in your view, most securely supported by the evidence you have studied.

A generic internal assessment mark scheme for assessing the understanding of how and why historical interpretations are created

AO2b	Generic Level Descriptors
Level 1 ↓	• Your answer demonstrates little understanding of historical debate or interpretation • Your answer tends to agree or disagree with the interpretation but has little support
Level 2 ↓	• Your answer demonstrates some understanding of a limited range of historical debate or interpretation • Your discussion of the interpretation is valid and you make reference to alternative interpretations, but they are not properly evaluated or explained
Level 3 ↓	• Your answer demonstrates good understanding of the nature of historical debate, discussing the interpretation in the context of one or more alternative interpretations • You begin to consider the interpretation in terms of the development of the historical debate that has taken place • You make some attempt to explain why the interpretations have been formed
Level 4	• Your answer demonstrates clear and consistent understanding of the nature of historical debate and a very good appreciation of how others have interpreted the past • The interpretations are placed into an historiographical context and you demonstrate an understanding of how and why the issues have been interpreted in different ways

Summary

The Do's and Don'ts when undertaking an internal assessment exercise:

DO

- Spell out the different interpretations linked to the topic under investigation and afford appropriate weighting to each of these viewpoints in your essay;

- Make sure you cover a range of sources – contemporary viewpoints, the views of historians, written accounts, oral testimonies, visual sources etc, which support the different interpretations to be discussed;

- Make sure each source is given a thorough evaluation in terms of its content value and its provenance – who said it, when and why did they say it?

- Make sure you link the interpretations to the key historians of that debate;

- Make sure you consider how the historian reached that particular viewpoint – the processes involved;

- Consider other factors that may have influenced the historian in reaching that viewpoint, such as political, nationalistic and religious factors;

- Make sure you demonstrate regular links back to the essay question;

- Conclude with a reasoned judgement and evaluation concerning the validity of the interpretation stated in the question.

DON'T

- Concentrate upon giving a narrative account by telling the story of the event;

- Concentrate too much upon one interpretation and ignore the other interpretations or afford them only superficial treatment;

- Carry out a superficial evaluation of the sources by concentrating solely upon their content value and ignoring their provenance;

- Ignore the historiography of the interpretation;

- Ramble off the point and include irrelevant information;

- Write well beyond the specified word limit;

- Fail to end your investigation with a reasoned conclusion linked back to the interpretation identified in the question.

CHAPTER FIVE

PREPARING FOR HISTORY EXAMINATIONS

Learning tips and revision techniques

I. Learning from past example: examining the comments made by Chief Examiners on candidate performances in external History examinations

One of the best methods of preparing for an external exam is to look over the reports produced by the Chief Examiners and examine the comments they have made upon the performance of past candidates. One of the striking features of such an exercise is that the same points of concern reappear year after year. Candidates continue to make the same basic mistakes, which could have been avoided with a little careful thought and pre-planning. Often the examiners will give tips in their report on how to answer particular styles of questions and give specific advice on how to improve performance, spelling out what you need to do to reach the top level of response.

The following comments are all taken from Chief Examiner Reports issued by the various Awarding Bodies on the performance by AS and A Level history candidates in the examinations each year.

General comments upon candidate performance

'Candidates _need to be better prepared_ for the requirements of the examination. They _need to have spent time looking at past papers_ to gain an appreciation of the style and requirements of answering particular styles of questions.' [2003]

'... further _attention to the assessment criteria_ would benefit candidates who frequently appear knowledgeable on the topic but are sometimes unable to maximise their marks.' [2005]

'My usual complaint about the _misspelling of the names_ of the historically famous still holds good.' [2006]

'Of some concern is the small but rather persistent number of scripts that continue to display _clear evidence of inadequate time management. It cannot be stressed often enough, of the importance which students should pay to the suggested allocation of time per question ... marks and very probably grades are being lost as a result of this problem.' [2008]

For discussion:
What are the key areas of concern identified by Chief Examiners in the above comments?

Comments upon essay writing skills

Many candidates showed reasonable knowledge and understanding but they often <u>failed to meet the precise demands of the questions</u>...' [1997]

'... some candidates <u>wrote copiously but far too generally.</u> At best, their answers were of a bland narrative type; at worst, irrelevant verbiage. Too often did examiners comment in the margin "irrelevant", "off the point", "far too general" or "this does not answer the question".' [1999]

'Candidates too <u>readily resort to narrative history rather than explanation</u> and their responses are too general, either lacking relevance to the question set, or the detailed knowledge to support a response on a specific aspect of the course.' [2002]

'Candidates <u>failed to offer complete coverage</u> of the whole period and so failed to gain full marks.' [2003]

'Some candidates were <u>unable to write two good essays</u>. Some produced a competent, well written first essay but could not sustain a second response. This may be because of a lack of essay practice, a lack of thorough preparation for the exam, or a time management problem.' [2004]

'Far too many candidates <u>failed to offer a clear judgement on the issues set</u> ... a common mistake being to dismiss the key factor in the question set and instead write on a range of other factors. Of equal concern are those candidates who discuss "To what extent..." by considering the main factor given and then going on to discuss other factors as well in a mechanical, listing fashion ... thereby <u>failing to assess the relative importance of each factor and coming to a well supported judgement.</u>' [2007]

For discussion:

(a)   What are the key failings of candidates when writing essays under examination conditions?

(b)   What are the strengths of good essay writing identified in the Chief Examiner's comments?

Comments upon source based questions

'There are still those who <u>concentrate too much on the content and insufficiently on the provenance.</u> Marks are still lost on the sections of the document-based questions by candidates <u>who do not accept the advice to "use in your answer relevant background knowledge".</u>' [2000]

'Many average candidates simply milk or re-hash the content of the sources to provide an answer. ... Candidates show three main weaknesses. Firstly, some seem uncertain of how to evaluate sources and _merely comment on their content;_ secondly, in assessing the value or reliability of a source, some candidates _fail to take into consideration the author's own prejudices when commenting on any possible bias or inaccuracy;_ thirdly, far too many candidates fail to take advantage of the opportunity to _use their own relevant background knowledge as well as information derived from other sources.'_ [2004]

'Candidates should be clear that it is not enough, when discussing the visual source, to make generalised comments about the problems of cartoons or illustrations as historical sources. What is needed is a _close analysis of content.'_ [2007]

> **For discussion:**
> (a) What are candidates not doing when asked to evaluate historical sources under examination conditions?
>
> (b) What practical advice would you give candidates about how to be successful in answering source based questions?

Comments upon historical interpretation questions

'Far too many candidates _rely on mechanistic responses_ and more alarmingly a significant number _fail to consider the attribution at all_ ... in some cases the comments on the attribution tended to be _rote learned and so formulaic_ that they could apply to any historian or author.' [2005]

'In many responses to this question the _historiographical aspects were not evident_ and the _source evaluation aspects were rather mechanistic,_ with little attempt to link them to the specific question set.' [2006]

'Far too many candidates lose marks by _failing to consider the validity of the interpretation presented against other possible interpretations,_ or _to consider the attribution by discussing the type of historian/author who made the interpretation,_ the methods available to that person, the date of publication and what evidence would be available at that time to make the interpretation.' [2008]

> **For discussion:**
> (a) What are candidates not doing when required to answer questions dealing with an evaluation of an historical interpretation?
>
> (b) What tips would you give a candidate attempting to evaluate the validity of an historical interpretation?

What do Chief Examiners not like to see on examination scripts?

(a)   Failing to answer the question

In the exam it is not just what you know but how you say it. It is important that you use what you know to argue a case that relates directly to the specific question you are asked. Too often examiners write 'Does not answer the question' on the script.

There could be a number of reasons why you might fail to answer the question correctly:

- Failing to address the command words in the question and thereby not answering the question that is being asked;

- Failing to recognise the meaning of particular words in the question. If there is a word/term that you are unsure of its meaning then you are best to avoid that question;

- Failing to pay attention to any dates provided for any period you are asked to discuss;

- Failing to be analytical and providing a narrative answer that ignores the arguments for and against a particular point;

- Making very generalised comments and failing to provide evidence to support the points you make in your essay;

- Failing to end your essay with a conclusion about the question asked in which you provide a reasoned judgement.

These are familiar enough points and they have been dealt with in some detail in chapters 2 and 3, there is nothing new here. You should be aware, however, that exam answers, although shorter and less detailed and structured than essays, are still judged using the same assessment criteria.

(b)   Failing to be selective

- You will never be asked to 'write all you know about...' but that is exactly what some candidates do when answering an essay question;

- The examiner does not want to know whether you can memorise a section of a book and repeat it. Rather they want to see that you can use the information you have acquired and select appropriate bits of it to answer a particular question – the material you include must be relevant;

- Not using parts of a source to support your answer or copying out large sections without being selective in your quotations;

- If you cram your answer full of facts, dates, names and quotations without placing them in the context of an argument and without selecting them for their relevance to that argument then the examiner will conclude that you do not understand what the question is asking.

(c) Using time badly

It is very common for candidates to manage their time badly under exam conditions, and thereby:

- Failing to finish the last essay;
- Failing to finish, or in many instances, start the last source based question;
- Resorting to bullet points because time has run out.

Remember that it is much easier to accumulate marks at the lower end of the scale than at the upper end, so it always makes sense to spend time on each question in direct proportion to its mark allocation.

(d) Poor presentation

Examiners often complain about answers that are:

- Unstructured, lacking an introduction or conclusion;
- Lacking any division into paragraphs;
- Written in note form rather than sentences;
- Written in unreadable handwriting;
- Failing to demonstrate a competent quality of written communication – candidates resort to using text language and other abbreviations.

2. Preparing for the external History examination

(a) Revising the course

Many students put off revision until the last minute and then panic when they realise that time is running out. Panic can make you think less clearly and it interferes with memory. It is important that you plan out a revision programme that spans the weeks prior to your first examination.

What do I need to know?	• You should start by making a list of all the content you need to know for the exam, then set about making a suitable timetable to accommodate your needs.
Active revision	• Your revision should be an active process, involving you doing something. You should avoid the mechanical reading of page after page in the false belief that it will all stick. It won't!
Make revision notes	• Revise with your pen in your hand. When you read over your notes you should make your own revision notes. These could include summary lists or key issues, in the form of numbered bullet points. Bullet points are much easier to remember than a paragraph of continuous prose.
Summarise	• By forcing your brain to decide what key issues to write down the process of prioritising and recording will have a greater retention rate than just aimless scanning over your notes.
Self-test	• Check how well your revision is going by self-testing. Up to 80% of new memorising is lost in the first twenty-four hours. It is therefore important that you revisit your notes on a regular basis, to reinforce and establish your learning of that topic.
Past exam papers	• Look over past exam papers. If questions appear on these papers that you cannot answer then your revision has not been thorough enough. It will enable you to get familiar with the language used and you may be able to spot a pattern in the topics that appear on the paper.
Selective revision	• Should I revise the whole course? You must be sensible and make a careful judgement about how selective your revision should be, based upon a careful study of past papers and the advice from your teacher. Remember that you should always have a fallback option should your chosen topics not appear in the paper.
Use of Internet	• Should I use the Internet for my revision? There are hundreds of Internet sites you can use for revision. However, you must not waste time online by visiting site after site, or by becoming distracted. It is easy to bow to the urge to check emails or to see if any friends are on MSM – this is time wasted.
Memory recall	• Find a method to facilitate the memorising of your notes which best suits your particular learning style. Many candidates find the use of mnemonics particularly helpful. This involves taking the first letter of a key word and using it to spell a particular term or word. Each of the key words should trigger the background details for that particular point.

Example: some candidates use **MAIN** as a mnemonic to remember the causes of the First World War.

MNEMONIC	KEY WORD	BACKGROUND DETAIL

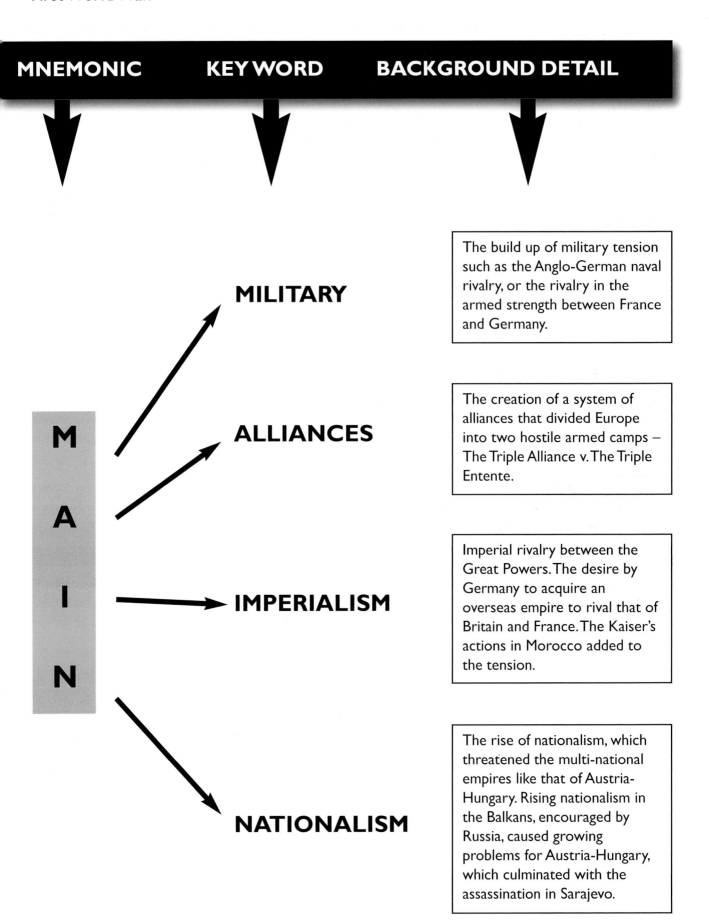

MILITARY

The build up of military tension such as the Anglo-German naval rivalry, or the rivalry in the armed strength between France and Germany.

ALLIANCES

The creation of a system of alliances that divided Europe into two hostile armed camps – The Triple Alliance v. The Triple Entente.

IMPERIALISM

Imperial rivalry between the Great Powers. The desire by Germany to acquire an overseas empire to rival that of Britain and France. The Kaiser's actions in Morocco added to the tension.

NATIONALISM

The rise of nationalism, which threatened the multi-national empires like that of Austria-Hungary. Rising nationalism in the Balkans, encouraged by Russia, caused growing problems for Austria-Hungary, which culminated with the assassination in Sarajevo.

M A I N

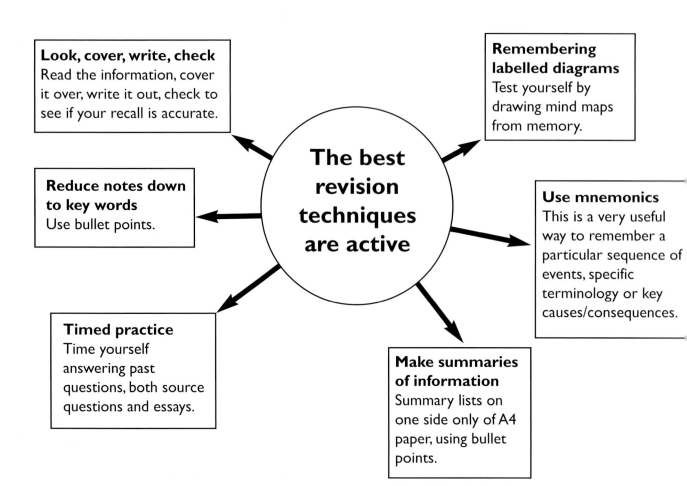

Look, cover, write, check
Read the information, cover it over, write it out, check to see if your recall is accurate.

Reduce notes down to key words
Use bullet points.

Timed practice
Time yourself answering past questions, both source questions and essays.

The best revision techniques are active

Remembering labelled diagrams
Test yourself by drawing mind maps from memory.

Use mnemonics
This is a very useful way to remember a particular sequence of events, specific terminology or key causes/consequences.

Make summaries of information
Summary lists on one side only of A4 paper, using bullet points.

Remember to factor in relaxation time between revision exercises.

Offer yourself rewards if you complete a section well.

Devising a structured revision programme	
A few months in advance	Sort out your notes – make sure they are complete. Fill in any gaps by obtaining the notes from either a friend or your teacher.
4 – 6 weeks in advance	Make summaries of your notes. List the key information on a single sided A4 sheet. Use diagrams and mnemonics to help recall.
1 – 2 weeks in advance	Test yourself to see if you can recall what is on your summary note sheets. Do some past questions under timed conditions. Go over the same material every few days to reinforce memory, continually self-testing.
1 – 2 days in advance	Use flash cards. Allow time for some relaxation, remembering to keep calm. After such a structured revision programme you should feel confident that you know the work and can enter the examination room well prepared. Aim to enjoy the examination – it is just a case of demonstrating your knowledge and understanding by writing down the required information in a particular order and sequence.

Template for your revision timetable:

Week	Main topic area	Individual topics to be revised
1		
2		
3		
4		
5		
6		
7		
8		
Exam		

REVISION TIPS

Start early.

Draft a timetable to map out what topic you will study each day.

Be realistic in what you plan to do each day – don't try to do too much.

Find a suitable venue to revise.

Be active in your revision – do not just sit on the bed and read your notes.

Summarise your notes, making headings for each topic and bullet points.

Spend longer on sections of the course you find most demanding and about which you are less confident.

Test yourself – answer questions from past papers under timed conditions.

(b)   Getting yourself 'geared up' during the final phase of revision

In the days immediately before your first examination you should be building up to a peak of preparation. You need to try to relax and get plenty of sleep. The hard work is over and you should by now be very familiar with the content. It is now only a matter of going over your summary notes, practising sketching out answers to questions and timing yourself.

(c) Mastering the examination itself

When you enter the examination room and are given the question paper you should:

Spend a few minutes looking over the paper:

- You must read the instructions carefully, paying attention to how many questions you are required to answer in each section of the paper;

- Apportion your time according to the mark allocation – you may find it useful to write out the timings for each question on the exam paper itself;

- When you have selected the question you are going to answer spend a little time brainstorming ideas. If it is an essay question circle or highlight the command words, write down some bullet points relating to the content, then number the bullet points to prioritise the order in which you will discuss them. If it is a document question underline the most important sections of the quotation as you read it, pay particular attention to the attribution, circle or highlight the key information such as the author, the book title, the year of publication and any relevant contextual information that is provided.

Make sure you answer the question that is set:

- Do not go off on a tangent, attempting to impress the examiner with the depth of your knowledge. If the information is not relevant to the question it will not score you marks and you will have wasted valuable time;

- Keep checking that what you have written actually answers the question by making regular links back to the question.

Answer the question in full:

- Make sure you answer all parts to the question; that you have covered the whole time period specified in the question; that you have spent sufficient time on each sub-question according to its mark allocation; remember to follow the structure that you have learnt – essays should have an introduction that outlines your interpretation of the question, an informed discussion and a reasoned conclusion in which you provide a judgement relating to the key issue of the question.

Be clear and legible:

- Explain your ideas clearly and in a logical fashion;

- Remember that the examiner has to be able to read your handwriting;

- Marks will be awarded for the quality of your written communication. You should answer using full sentences and avoid any abbreviations or text language. The names of key historical persons, places and events should be spelt correctly.

Budget your time accordingly:

- Allocate time in direct proportion to the percentage of total marks. Do not go beyond the apportioned time because this will seriously reduce your chances of scoring high marks in the remaining questions;

- Remember that you do not have to answer questions consecutively. You can if you wish start with question 4, for instance, if that is a topic area you are most confident with, and then go back to a previous question;

- Stay in control. Keep calm, jot down your initial thoughts, arrange them into an appropriate order and proceed to answer the question at a steady pace. Do not go into panic mode because the question is worded differently from what you are used to;

- Allow a few minutes at the end to check over your answers looking for grammatical and punctuation faults and for any obvious spelling mistakes.

Common faults when writing under examination conditions

- Not defining or explaining key terms;
- Not backing up your arguments with specific historical evidence;
- Using historical information but missing the point of the question;
- Failing to draw conclusions where relevant;
- Misappropriation of the time – unable to finish the paper.

EXAMINATION TIPS

Arrive in plenty of time.

Be positive – keep calm and breathe deeply.

Read the paper through before you start to write, paying particular attention to the number of questions you are expected to answer.

Make a reasoned choice about which questions to answer, making sure you can answer all the relevant sub-questions.

Apportion your time according to the mark allocation for each sub-question – do not go over the allocated time.

Complete all the required questions.

Remember to apply all the appropriate techniques for answering particular styles of question – evaluating sources and addressing the attribution, answering open ended or structured essays, addressing historical interpretations.

Stick to the point and answer the questions in full.

Allow time at the end to read over your answers, making any necessary corrections or additions.

Give of your best throughout the whole examination.

(d) Post examination

Too often after the examination candidates get unduly concerned about what they did or did not write in answer to the questions. There is always a tendency for you to dwell on the negatives – you left out this or forgot to make a link between two factors. Such lengthy post-mortems serve no purpose and they can be bad for you. If you made an obvious mistake then simply take a mental note of it and vow not to repeat it in your next examination. Once the exam is over you need to forget it and concentrate upon preparing for the next one.

How prepared will you be for the final history examinations?

Case studies of candidates taking AS/A Level history examinations

Jack fails to take the workload seriously

- The exams will commence in a few days time and Jack has only just started to revise;

- He has gaps in his class notes but he has made no attempt to copy up what is missing and so his knowledge is incomplete and patchy;

- His knowledge of particular topics is very limited and he has narrowed down his choice of essay topics to just a bare minimum. He is hoping the right questions come up;

- He has sat a mock paper but has not used it to reflect upon what went well and what his weak areas were;

- He has done some past questions but has made no serious attempt to estimate what might come up on the paper and he is just revising the few topics he likes;

- He does not manage his time well in the exams and he has failed to get on to answering some questions in past exams;

- He has missed out parts of a question in the past.

For discussion:
What advice would you give Jack to ensure that he does better in future examinations?

Charlotte is well prepared and feels confident

- Charlotte has been systematically revising over a long period and is now in a position where she can ease off in the immediate run up to her first exam;

- She has a very comprehensive set of class notes together with additional notes she has made during the year from which to compile her revision notes;

- She has set herself a realistic revision timetable and has stuck to it;

- She has sat several mock exam papers under timed conditions and she is aware of what needs to be done and how much time to allow to do it;

- She has gone over her class notes as well as previous essays she has written and taken note of her teacher's comments, and she has attempted to spot exam questions;

- She has practised every type of essay question;

- She is strict in allocating time during the exam according to the percentage of marks allocated to each question;

- She reads the question carefully, annotates the sources, scribbles brief notes to help draft a plan and ticks off those points as she mentions them in her answer;

- She keeps a regular check to see if what she writes answers the question;

- She attempts all the required number of questions;

- She always allows time at the end to check over her answers.

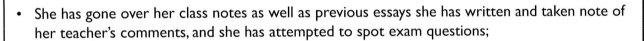

For discussion:
To what extent does your work ethos and revision programme replicate that of Charlotte?

Elin lacks confidence and easily gets into a panic

- Elin has a good set of class notes and she has undertaken the required background reading advised by her teacher;

- Whenever she sits down and attempts to begin the revision process her stomach churns and she gets into a panic and has to leave the work;

- She has drafted a revision timetable but finds it difficult to stick to it;

- Much of her revision consists of just reading and re-reading her class notes, and consequently she tends to lose concentration;

- She has answered some past questions but only managed to sit one of the two mock papers;

- She is not very good at predicting questions and will attempt to learn everything;

- In the past she has not been able to finish the exams as she runs out of time to complete the last section of the paper;

- She has a tendency to go to pieces in the run-up to the exams and gets very worked up prior to taking the exam itself;

- Her teacher is of the opinion she has the ability to attain a high grade but her feeling of insecurity and not being in control usually precludes her giving of her best.

For discussion:
What advice would you give Elin mid-way through Year 13 to ensure that she avoids the pitfalls listed in her profile above?

These three case studies have served to illustrate the range of candidates who will sit their final history examination. Some will enter the examination room feeling confident, knowing that they have prepared in a thorough fashion over a long period. Others will enter with the false belief that their last minute dash to learn their notes will be sufficient to see them successfully through the examinations and secure them a reasonable grade. A small number will lack confidence and will enter the exam room as a bag of nerves. They may well be very able candidates but their negative thought patterns will have hindered their revision programme.

What is required is a balance between a rigorous and efficient revision programme, intermixed with regular and rewarding relaxation time, which will facilitate the right mental state to induce learning. **Emotional well-being is just as important as mental well-being** but candidates often ignore it. You will not be able to learn your work if your brain is in panic mode. You need to ensure that you are relaxed and find a suitable venue and ambiance that suits your particular learning style. That might mean having music played in the background or a completely silent venue. Getting the balance right between work and play is the key to success.

WHICH ONE ARE YOU?

For discussion:

(a)   Having read the three case studies, which one best matches your current status in terms of work ethos and emotional well-being?

(b)   What do you need to do to ensure that you are adequately prepared for the terminal examinations?

Extending your study – aiming for the A* grade

The candidates who perform best at A Level are those who are in command of their chosen topics. They possess a depth of knowledge and understanding that allows them to place events into a wider historical perspective, draw comparisons and identify similarities and differences, identify periods of change and continuity and provide a range of reasons to explain such factors, and communicate their ideas in a clear, methodical and sophisticated manner.

Such candidates often feel the urge to read more extensively and sometimes outside their chosen topic areas. Indeed, this is one of the key characteristics of an A* candidate, a willingness to undertake independent and further research which goes beyond the scope of what is discussed in the classroom.

Reading historical journals and magazines are a good method of improving your skills in this subject as they offer:

- A range of authoritative articles on varied historical topics covering all time periods;
- Useful advice on historical skills and methods;
- The most up to date research on topical issues;
- Articles that deal with issues of historiography;
- Book reviews;
- Web-site reviews.

Examples of monthly historical magazines: **History Magazine** [BBC publishing]
History Today [Historical Association]
Modern History Review [Philip Allan Updates]

The more advanced might want to consider the theoretical side of history and would be advised to read such works as:

What is History? by E. H. Carr
The practice of History by G. R. Elton
The pursuit of History by John Tosh

These works consider the broader questions that have been touched upon in this book. They consider how the historian operates and investigates the past, they examine the types of evidence available to the historian and consider how to handle such source material, and they investigate the process of historical interpretation and the importance of historiography. These are the skills that will form the basis of your study of history at university.

What have you gained from this study guide?

The aim of this study guide has been to deliver practical advice to you, the student of AS/A Level history, on how to get the most out of your history course and how best to prepare yourself for the examinations. Throughout this guide you have been given specific advice on:

- How the historian sets about investigating the past and on the research methods to adopt;
- How to structure and write history essays;
- How to tackle the source analysis and evaluation questions;
- How to deal effectively and purposely with historical interpretations;
- How to best prepare for the examinations, whether it is at the end of Year 12 or Year 13.

It is now up to you to reflect upon the suggestions and advice that has been given upon these topic areas. You can adopt those that best suit your particular learning style and experiment with others. To get the best out of this book you should not just read it once and say done that, finished with that. Rather, you should flick through it periodically and hone in on the areas that you are currently working on, whether it be essay writing or dealing with historical interpretation. It is intended to be a working document that you can constantly keep by your side as you journey through the AS/A Level course.